PROCLAMATION:
Aids for Interpreting the Lessons of the Church Year

LESSER FESTIVALS 2

Philip Pfatteicher

FORTRESS PRESS   Philadelphia, Pennsylvania

General Preface

Proclamation: Aids for Interpreting the Lessons of the Church Year is a series of twenty-six books designed to help clergymen carry out their preaching ministry. It offers exegetical interpretations of the lessons for each Sunday and many of the festivals of the church year, plus homiletical ideas and insights.

The basic thrust of the series is ecumenical. In recent years the Episcopal church, the Roman Catholic church, the United Church of Christ, the Christian Church (Disciples of Christ), and the Lutheran and Presbyterian churches have adopted lectionaries that are based on a common three-year system of lessons for the Sundays and festivals of the church year. *Proclamation* grows out of this development, and authors have been chosen from all of these traditions. Some of the contributors are parish pastors; others are teachers, both of biblical interpretation and of homiletics. Ecumenical interchange has been encouraged by putting two persons from different traditions to work on a single volume, one with the primary responsibility for exegesis and the other for homiletical interpretation.

Despite the high percentage of agreement between the traditions, both in the festivals that are celebrated and the lessons that are appointed to be read on a given day, there are still areas of divergence. Frequently the authors of individual volumes have tried to take into account the various textual traditions, but in some cases this has proved to be impossible; in such cases we have felt constrained to limit the material to the Lutheran readings.

The preacher who is looking for "canned sermons" in these books will be disappointed. These books are one step removed from the pulpit: they explain what the lessons are saying and suggest ways of relating this biblical message to the contemporary situation. As such they are springboards for creative thought as well as for faithful proclamation of the word.

The present volume is one of two volumes on the Lesser Festivals written by Philip H. Pfatteicher. Dr. Pfatteicher is Professor of English and Lutheran Campus Pastor at East Stroudsburg (Pennsylvania) State College. He is a pastor of the Lutheran Church in America who has served parishes in Philadelphia and in the Bronx, and he is the author of articles and reviews in a number of publications. He is also a member of the Liturgical Text Committee of the Inter-Lutheran Commission on Worship and has served as chairman of the subcommittee on the Marriage Service (*Contemporary Worship 3*) and on the Calendar (*Contemporary Worship 6*) and is now chairman of the subcommittee on the Divine Office.

Introduction

The evolution of the church year is popularly thought to have begun with the observance of the major events of Christ's life—Christmas, Easter, Pentecost—and then the other times and seasons were gradually filled in to complete the year. Later still, it is sometimes thought, other days were added which cluttered the original straightforward pattern of the year. But in fact the keeping of saints' days and the church year developed together. The New Testament makes reference to the celebration and observance of the first day of the week as the Lord's Day (Rev. 1:10), the day of resurrection. In addition, from very early times, before the church year developed, particular days were kept as the anniversaries of the deaths of martyrs, who followed Jesus in giving up their lives for the kingdom (cf. Rev. 6:9; 17:6). While Paul (2 Cor. 1:1; Eph. 1:1; Phil. 1:1; Col. 1:1) often uses the word "saint" to mean all believers, all the members of the holy nation of the church, "those sanctified in Christ Jesus" (1 Cor. 1:2), he also at times suggests that sainthood is a vocation not yet completed (e.g., "God's beloved in Rome who are called to be saints"—Rom. 1:7). In the Book of Revelation the term seems to be moving toward being restricted to those of the believers who have died and so achieved a share in Christ's victory (Rev. 14:13) and also to a still more select group within the church ("saints, apostles, and prophets"—18:20). The confessors seem to have been honored next—those who acknowledged Christ before the world not by dying but by a kind of death such as imprisonment or exile. Others worthy of mention were added in succeeding centuries and the calendar was lengthened.

At the time of the Reformation both the Lutheran and the Anglican reformers vastly simplified the church year by cutting away all the clutter of saints' days that had proliferated beyond control so that every day of the year had several saints associated with it. The reformers kept only the days of the twelve Apostles and the four evangelists as those days beyond all doubt worth keeping (perhaps partly on the mistaken assumption that these were the original days). Certain other popular days remained on various Lutheran calendars into the nineteenth century. Recent Roman Catholic calendars have drastically simplified their calendar, and the Anglicans and the Lutherans have modestly enriched theirs. All three churches indicate a common understanding of the year and its days.

It is important to remember that Sunday and saints' days developed side by side, for, like Sunday, saints' days are basically a celebration of the Easter mystery extended through the year and given particular focus in certain individuals. These days tell of the suffering and the glorification of Christ as well as the suffering and the glorification of those who live in him. The saints are conspicuous examples of those who have achieved full maturity and who are transparent to the grace of God which worked in them.

There are included here also a few other days commemorating events rather than people, and these are associated with that other mystery of the Christian year, the Incarnation. These are the Presentation, the Annunciation, the Visitation, the Nativity of John the Baptizer—festivals of Christ in his coming into the world. So the Incarnation is also extended through the year and held constantly before the memory of the church.

All the Lesser Festivals in the Lutheran calendar, which parallel closely those of the Episcopal calendar and which are all present (except for Reformation Day) on the new Roman Catholic calendar, are included in these two volumes. To this list were added Thanksgiving Day and National Holiday because of their importance in the civil calendar. Most of the lessons have been already dealt with exegetically in the previous volumes of this series, and cross-references are provided here to facilitate the reader's referring to them. The comments here for each day are intended to summarize the critical understanding of the texts with reference to their relation to the particular day on which they are read. The preacher's task remains to apply these texts to the individual situation of the congregation.

Moreover, while these comments are based on the Lutheran calendar and lectionary, they take into account all the readings suggested by the three Western traditions which have a calendar of lesser festivals (Lutheran, Roman Catholic, Episcopal). Examining these three lectionaries together has proved to be, to this author at least, a rewarding experience, and it is hoped that some of the reward of this comparison might be felt by the reader. In using the three lectionaries for the holy days together, a new understanding both of the richness of Scripture and the reasons for these particular choices emerges and suggests something of the wealth of the possibilities for proclaiming the significance of these festival days. The outlook of one tradition is expanded and enriched by an examination of the others, much as the three-year cycle of readings enriches the proclamation on the Sundays and major festivals of the year.

Table of Contents

St. Mary Magdalene (July 22) — 1

St. James the Elder, Apostle (July 25) — 5

Mary, Mother of Our Lord (August 15) — 9

St. Bartholomew, Apostle (August 24) — 12

Holy Cross Day (September 14) — 16

St. Matthew, Apostle and Evangelist (September 21) — 21

St. Michael and All Angels (September 29) — 25

St. Luke, Evangelist (October 18) — 28

St. Simon and St. Jude, Apostles (October 28) — 33

Reformation Day (October 31) — 37

All Saints' Day (November 1) — 41

Thanksgiving Day — 46

National Holiday — 50

St. Mary Magdalene

JULY 22

Lutheran	*Roman Catholic*	*Episcopal*
Ruth 1:6–18* or	Song of Sol. 3:1–4a	Acts 13:27–31†
Exod. 2:1–10		2 Cor. 5:14–18‡
Acts 13:26–33a†		John 20:11–18§
John 20:1–2, 11–18§	John 20:1–2, 11–18§	

Luke 8:1–2 says that from Mary Magdalene "seven demons had gone out" and that she then accompanied Jesus in Galilee. She was present at the crucifixion (Mark 15:40) and the tomb (Mark 16:1) and was the first to see the risen Christ (Mark 16:9; John 20:11–18), and she was the first to bear the news of the resurrection to the Apostles. She has been called, therefore, the "apostle to the Apostles." Whenever the Gospels list the women who were with Jesus, Mary Magdalene is listed first (John 19:25 is the sole exception), perhaps because she was the first to see Jesus. In the Western tradition she has been identified with the woman "who was a sinner" (Luke 7:37–50)—she, unlike anyone else in Christian calendars, bears the title "Penitent"—but there is no evidence to support the identification. She has also been identified with Mary, the sister of Martha of Bethany (Luke 10:38–42; John 12:3). The Western church has, however, generally come to accept the tradition of the East that these are three different persons, and recent calendars have emphasized her primary role as witness to the resurrection.

The *First Lesson:* It will take some doing on the part of the preacher to apply the readings from the OT to Mary Magdalene. Ruth 1:6–18 presents the ministry of a young woman to her mother-in-law and to the whole people of Israel as she teaches them the size and the greatness of God's love. Although Naomi is prominent in the story, the central figure is Ruth. She is able to overcome her natural loyalty to her own land and people and accept as her own Naomi's land and house and God. The seal and proof of her determination is her declaration that she will die and

* see Pentecost 21, Series C   ‡ see Pentecost 5, Series B
† see Easter 4, Series A   § see Resurrection, Series A (alt.)

lay down her bones in Naomi's land and so be one with her new God (whom she calls Yahweh) and land and people. Ruth exemplifies the surpassingly excellent way of love (1 Corinthians 13) that, while it flies in the face of common sense, nonetheless at times can see and feel more surely than the mind. It was Ruth who was the great-grandmother of David and the ancestor of Jesus. The preacher might, perhaps, careful not to overstate the case, draw a parallel between Ruth's "not even death will part me from you" and Mary Magdalene's deeper discovery of the union of the believer and her Lord.

Exod. 2:1–10 also tells of one bound both to the old and to the new. Moses is adopted by a princess of Egypt but is nursed by a Hebrew mother. But the central figure for this day is the tender and sensitive princess, who, though an Egyptian, fears God and disobeys her father's edict by preserving the infant Moses and so insures the continuation of the people of Israel and their eventual return to their land. Though herself of the old, she nonetheless played a decisive role in bringing the new. What seemed to be chance was providence. Similarly, Mary Magdalene is an important link between the old and the new, between Jesus' death and Jesus' resurrection.

The Roman Catholic lesson, Song of Sol. 3:1–4a, is a woman's dream of a restless search for her lover until she finds him. To fit this festival, the poem must be understood allegorically and probably applied to Mary Magdalene's quest for God who satisfies the soul; in great distress with the "seven demons," she at last finds Jesus before dawn at the tomb and rejoices in the possession.

The Episcopal lectionary does well by following the pattern of Easter and taking the First Lesson from the Book of Acts. In the Lutheran lectionary it is the **Second Lesson**. The key phrase for this festival is surely v. 31, Jesus "appeared to those who came up with him from Galilee to Jerusalem, who are now his witnesses to the people." Mary Magdalene's claim to commemoration is that she is a principal witness to the resurrection. The passage is the heart of Paul's first work in Asia Minor and the only full length report of a Pauline sermon that we possess. He gave the address at the synagogue at Pisidian Antioch (a Roman colony and military center) on a Sabbath, as was his custom. It is a sample, probably composed by Luke to represent the thrust of the Pauline sermon, and a typical sermon a Christian preacher of the time would address to a Hellenistic-Jewish congregation. Had this been an actual transcription of Paul's words, one would expect to find a reference to his own encounter with the risen Lord. The witnesses are not only in Jerusalem: one is standing before the congregation in Antioch. Notable in this particular formulation is the address to both Jews and God-fearing Gentiles who share the message of salvation, the emphasis on the innocence of Jesus, the fulfillment of the Scriptures which are read weekly in the synagogues, and the living witness to the risen Savior. Despite his people's rejection, God has kept his promise, and the whole race has been rescued. Such is the kerygma according to Paul as rendered by Luke; it is the same message as that of Peter (Acts 2) and of Stephen (Acts 7).

When God fulfilled his old promises at last—according to his sure plan—humankind was not ready for the fulfillment and could not recognize it. It was true of the ministry of Jesus; it is also true, we know, of the preaching of the resurrection. Many were unable to hear and unable to see. Those who were prepared by fulfilling their ordinary responsibilities and by waiting and hoping through the long darkness, never forgetting the promise, were able to hear and see when Jesus came. And when dull men crucified him, there were still some who waited and hoped even in that darkness, against all sense and reason, that still God's promise held good and that still his will would be done. And so the women—first one woman alone, Mary Magdalene, according to John—came to the tomb before dawn and saw the world-shattering evidence of resurrection: an empty tomb and angels, but most of all, Jesus himself. In the darkness before the dawn, Jesus met them, and the rising light began its dawn as the sun "which goes not down."

The message of fulfillment, victory, and salvation is most of all not the words of a book nor formulations of doctrine but is the living testimony of those who have seen and heard, who have themselves encountered the risen Lord in his saving power to make free and to make whole. Mary, out of whom went seven demons. knew his power in her life before he died, and after the crucifixion she waited for the rest of the story which she knew had to come. And come it did as Jesus himself came to her. Condemning Jesus, those who rejected him unwittingly fulfilled God's plan declared by the prophets (cf. the First Lesson: pharaoh).

The **Gospel:** In the conclusion of the Fourth Gospel, before the epilogue (chap. 21), there are three basic events: the introductory fact of the empty tomb and two parallel appearances of Jesus, first to Mary Magdalene and then to the ten and to Thomas. Each appearance includes a confession of faith and a view to those yet to learn the news of salvation. As the Gospel began with a renewal of creation, so the Gospel ends with a restoration of the fall: a woman and then a man renew and deepen their faith in what God has done. (And Jesus is the gardener.)

"While it was still dark" (cf. the synoptic emphasis on dawn), Mary Magdalene came to the tomb and found it empty. Once again in the Fourth Gospel the theme of darkness is apparent (cf. 1:5; 3:1–2; 13:30), representing ignorance and hostility. In the dark, Magdalene, as yet ignorant of the resurrection, is terrified by the empty tomb and weeps because she thinks the body has been stolen. The empty tomb meant that Jesus was elsewhere, but in accordance with the Johannine theme of misunderstanding she sees the figure of Jesus come to her (presumably not yet looking directly at him) and does not yet recognize him. He speaks and she does not recognize the voice. In her loving impetuosity she offers to do something with the body. (How could she do it alone?) Then, at last, he calls her by name, and she knows the sound and turns and knows him (cf. 10: 3) and makes her confession, "Rabboni" (cf. 1:38)—a solemn form of the more usual "rabbi" and used chiefly of God. "Rabbi" in John is frequently preliminary to greater titles (cf. 1:38 ff.; 3:2 ff.), but John's explanation of the word ("which means Teacher") plays down the parallelism with Thomas' confession which follows. The name suggests the dawn of faith: stronger than the "rabbi" of 1:38, but less than Thomas' "My Lord and my God."

Mary reaches out to embrace Jesus but is forbidden from doing so by Jesus, for she seems to want to take up the relationship where it ended before the crucifixion. Jesus, however, wants to emphasize the newness of the risen life and to suggest that there is more to come. The ascension in John's chronology is to take place later that morning and so too is the gift of the Spirit which makes people God's children. Mary must not hinder the completion of the glorification. Time cannot stand still; there is yet more to come. The relationship between Jesus and the disciples is not merely resumed but renewed by the resurrection. As Ruth's adoption of Naomi's people and God (First Lesson) suggests, Jesus here is declaring his solidarity with his disciples who now become children of the Father (1:12; 3:5).

The reading concludes with Mary telling the disciples, "I have seen the Lord." The risen Jesus has become the Lord, the gardener indeed, for he is no less than God himself. Christ has found her who sought him and she sees him with the eyes of faith.

St. James the Elder, Apostle

JULY 25

Lutheran	*Roman Catholic*	*Episcopal*
1 Kings 19:9–18*		Jer. 45
Acts 11:27–12:3a	2 Cor. 4:7–15†	Acts 11:27–12:2
Mark 10:35–45‡	Matt. 20:20–28§	Matt. 20:20–28§

Big James, as opposed to "little James" who is commemorated with Philip on May 1, was a fisherman and brother of John. They were the two "sons of thunder" (or wrath or tumult) because of their stormy temperaments or perhaps because they were Zealots or counter-revolutionaries (Mark 3:17; cf. Mark 9:38, Luke 9:54–55). But the title "sons of thunder" is closely connected with the cult of twins and may imply either that James and John were twins or that all of the twelve were called in pairs. James and John together with Peter formed the inner, privileged group of disciples who were present at the transfiguration, the raising of Jairus' daughter, the agony in Gethsemane. James' martyrdom is reported in Acts 12:2. He is the only Apostle whose death is recorded in Scripture; he was beheaded by Herod Agrippa I, grandson of Herod the Great, near Easter around 42–44. The shrine of Santiago de Compostella in Spain, which was thought to house the body of James after his death in Jerusalem, was one of the great centers of pilgrimage throughout the Middle Ages.

The *First Lesson:* Ahab, who was ruler of the northern kindom of Israel, had cemented an old alliance with Tyre by marrying Jezebel, the daughter of their king (16:31). Ahab then introduced the worship of Astarte and Baalism which included human sacrifice (16:34). However, Elijah on Mt. Carmel routed the priests of Baal (18:20–46) in the contest between Yahweh and Baal and had them slain. The danger of an alien religion seemed over; the long drought was broken by rain. But Jezebel, unmoved by Yahweh's power, threatened Elijah's life, and he fled to the southernmost town of the southern kingdom. Leaving his servant, Elijah went into the desert, disconsolate in his disappointment. His best work seemed a failure. He lived for a time in a cave on Mt. Horeb (cf. Judg.

* see Pentecost 12, Series A   ‡ see Pentecost 23, Series B
† see Pentecost 2 and 3, Series B   § see Lent 4, Series A

5:4; Hab. 3:3), far down in the Sinai wallowing in his bitterness. There, where Moses had seen God (Exod. 33:17–23), Elijah gains a new understanding of himself and of God. Yahweh comes to him and asks with reproach, "What are you doing here?" (cf. 17:18). With an easy answer, Elijah dismisses all the people of Israel as faithless and pictures himself alone as zealous for the Lord and persecuted for it. God's reply is to display all the traditional phenomena of a theophany—wind and earthquake and fire—yet they were but precursors of the presence which came in a whisper of light breeze or perhaps, following the Hebrew, "a sound of gentle stillness," an eerie silence. Into this awesome stillness God came to his prophet with a message of violence and of shame—the king whom Elijah is to anoint will slaughter those who have gone after other gods; and to silence Elijah's proud claim to be the last faithful survivor of the religion of Yahweh, God tells Elijah that he is but one of seven thousand who have not worshiped Baal. God's vengeance is terrible and the vastness of his resources is unperceived. The remnant is larger than Elijah imagined; far more people than Elijah have been troubled by recent events, and a successor has been provided.

The Episcopal First Lesson, Jeremiah 45, is Jeremiah's oracle to his secretary, Baruch, in a time when civilization itself seemed to be breaking up. Everything had failed, ordinary things and great things alike seemed empty. Yet God is God (cf. the Gospel), and his protection abides even though all else is broken.

While the **Second Lesson** is a natural one for St. James' Day, since it tells of his martyrdom, there are problems in understanding it. (The Roman Catholic lectionary has changed the traditional reading to 2 Cor. 4:7–15.) The lesson is difficult to correlate with what Paul in his letters tells of his work (Gal. 1–2). Some suggest the reading is a doublet of Acts 15:2–29 and 21:10–11. Moreover, chap. 12 seems clumsily fitted into its context.

The visit to Jerusalem seems to have been Paul's first introduction to the church at Jerusalem. During the reign of Claudius (A.D. 41–54) there were several famines, one of the worst of which in Judea occurred in A.D. 46. (There was no known world-wide famine during the reign of Claudius.) Christians, especially those who had given away all their possessions (Acts 2:45), would not be found eligible for Jewish relief funds and so would bear a disproportionate share of the suffering. The famine had been predicted by the prophet Agabus.

According to Eph. 2:20, the church is built upon apostles and prophets, that is, the witnesses to Jesus' ministry and resurrection, and upon the charismatics who were the NT prophets who normally occupy second place after the apostles (1 Cor. 12:28). The apostles were witnesses to Jesus and preached the kerygma; the prophets were witnesses to the Spirit and communicated his message (cf. 1 Cor. 14:6, 26, 30; Eph. 3:5). These NT prophets sometimes foretell the future as they do here (see Acts 21:10–11), sometimes speaking new languages, sometimes building up and consoling (1 Cor. 14:3). Their principal role seems to have been, under the guidance of the Spirit, to open up the meaning of the OT Scripture, especially the OT prophets (Eph. 3:5), and explain the mystery kept secret for long ages (Rom. 16:25).

The disciples at Antioch, a wealthy city of the Empire, which had apparently become the center of Christianity, were moved by the prophets from Jerusalem to send a contribution to the elders of the Jerusalem church (the Apostles were apparently no longer there) by the hands of Barnabas, the most honored representative of Hellenistic Christianity, and Paul. For Jerusalem both by its location and by its poverty would suffer acutely in the coming famine.

The opportunity for the preacher to draw parallels with the hunger of the modern world is plain and urgent. When people are hungry, it is the responsibility of the church to be an agent of relief, and the responsibility of those who are comparatively well off is to share with those who have less.

The persecution under Herod, dated vaguely by Luke "about this time," surely occurred before the preceding passage, since Herod Agrippa died in A.D. 44. Herod was popular with the Jews for he meticulously kept the law, and his careful cultivation of popular favor was the cause of his attack on the leaders of the church. There is some reason to believe that John, who is not mentioned again in Acts, was also killed with his brother James in this persecution (cf. the prediction in Mark 10:39). Two early calendars commemorate James and John together on December 27.

The success of the execution of James encouraged Herod to arrest Peter also, but, ever punctilious, he delayed Peter's trial until the end of Passover. No effort was made by the Apostles to replace James, as was done with Judas, for James was understood to have gone by martyrdom to his heavenly throne (Matt. 19:28; Luke 22:28–30). Judas by betrayal had forfeited his.

The Roman Catholic reading, 2 Cor. 4:7–15, is a general passage on the ministry of an Apostle, specifically Paul, but it is easily extended to include the work of the twelve and to include the life of all who bear the name of Christ. Affliction reveals the grace and power of God.

In the *Gospel*, Jesus has just announced (for the third time as Mark tells it) his impending death (10:33–34). Naturally, perhaps, the Apostles did not understand the significance of what Jesus was telling them. This reading reveals the depths of their ignorance of the ways of God and of what lay ahead not only for Jesus but for them as well. The brothers James and John, true to the implications of their epithet "sons of thunder," in their selfishness approach Jesus with a request for special favor. Mark's presumably older account presents the event baldly: to forestall the others, James and John ask Jesus for a commitment to give them whatever they ask, namely, to sit in honor at his right and left hand in the future messianic kingdom (Matt. 20:21), assuming the arrival of that reign was immanent, to be inaugurated perhaps upon their arrival in Jerusalem, the royal city. (Perhaps they envisioned thrones of judgment— Matt. 19:28—or glory at the messianic banquet—14:25). Matthew's account softens the bluntness of the request and puts it in the mouth of the brothers' mother, although Jesus' answer is directed to the brothers whose request it actually is.

Jesus rebukes them in their total misunderstanding, saying bluntly, "You do not know what you are asking." Further, he elicits from them an indication of their willingness to share his future. He speaks of baptism (Matthew omits this reference) and the cup—symbols of the impending passion. Baptism (by immersion) suggests drowning in overwhelming disaster (Ps. 42:7; 69:2; 124:4; Isa. 43:2; Luke 12:50) and the cup is the chalice of suffering (Ps. 75:8; Isa. 51:17, 22; Jer. 25: 15–18; Luke 22:20; John 18:11; Heb. 9:15). In addition, in the context of the state of the young church, the warning was heard in these words that those who were baptized into Christ and who shared the eucharistic cup were pledging themselves to a life that might well involve martyrdom. This way was a dangerous way, and the fainthearted were warned .

The preacher should not too easily assume that Jesus' reference is to the martyrdom of James and John. Calamity, tribulation, and a share in the messianic suffering are to be their lot to be sure, but these may or may not involve a martyr's death. The traditional assumption that John died a natural death in old age may well be so, and Jesus' saying can mean death for James but not necessarily for John. So the text speaks to all.

The two Apostles answer with incredible ease and optimism, "We are able," grasping at what cannot be had without pain and death. One is reminded of Joshua 24, where God's spokesman insistently urges the people to consider carefully whether they want to bind themselves to an uncomfortable way of life and perhaps also of death. The other ten understand no more than the brothers, and in their own way the ten are as selfish as James and John and as quick to announce their ability to do what Jesus is about to do, not weighing the implications of being associated with the work of God. Not until one loses the sense of self-concern is one able to go in the way of the cross as a servant and as a slave. And there is no earthly glory in that.

James (and John too if one is to accept the full force of Jesus' saying) will soon know what it is to share the cup of suffering and the baptism of death. But beyond lie the cup of joy (Ps. 23:5; 116:13; Jer. 16:7) and the rebirth of resurrection. The disciple must be careful when he prays, for the prayer might be answered and it might not be as one expects. The glory is not obtained by death but by God's gift, and so the characteristic question a disciple asks is not what can I get, but what can I give?

St. James, as this Gospel shows, was no "saint" in the popular understanding of the word. He was, like the other eleven, an ordinary man with failings and weaknesses who nevertheless by the grace of God changed the world. Even the Apostles' blindness and their arrogance was made to serve God's purpose.

Mary, Mother of Our Lord

AUGUST 15

Lutheran	*Roman Catholic*	*Episcopal*
Isa. 61:7–11	Rev. 11:19a; 12:1–6a, 10ab	Isa. 61:7–11
Gal. 4:4–7*	1 Cor. 15:20–26†	Gal. 4:4–7*
Luke 1:46–55‡	Luke 1:39–56‡	Luke 1:46–55‡

From the biblical record nothing is known of Mary's birth or parentage or death. But more is known about her than about most of the Apostles. The NT shows Mary present at all the important events of her son's life: the birth cycle, the first miracle at Cana, at the cross, at the tomb, waiting with the Apostles for the gift of the Spirit. There are representations of her in the catacombs from the first half of the second century. Since early times, beginning in the East, August 15 has been observed as the day of her "falling asleep," i.e., her death (cf. Acts 7:60). Through the centuries, Mary has been a principal focus of devotional attention:

* see Christmas 1, Series A   ‡ see Advent 4, Series C
† see Last Pentecost, Series A

chosen by God as his servant, the one from whom Jesus took his flesh, the God-bearer, the personification of the old Israel and of the new, obedient to the word of God.

The *First Lesson* is a magnificat by Zion praising God's restoration of her joy. The first verse is said by the prophet and recalls 40:2, the comfort to a people long without consolation. Yahweh speaks next (vv. 8–9) asserting his love of justice and his faithfulness and promising eternal blessing. The everlasting covenant God makes with his people is one that will increase in splendor and renown from children to children, generation to generation. This lasting and increasing glory will lead the nations to acknowledge Yahweh's blessing of his people. The promises to Abraham (Gen. 12:2) are at last fulfilled.

In the final two verses (10–11) Zion herself is heard celebrating the fulfillment of love between her and God. The word of God is as good as fulfilled. His promise is sufficient for his people to treat the announced gifts as accomplished fact. Festal garments and the robe of righteousness, as opposed to garments of vengeance and fury worn by Yahweh (59:17), show the gladness of the restored people who rejoice with the joy of a wedding. Yahweh has married his people, and they look forward to the consummation. Desolation has been replaced with gladness, death by life, despair by hope.

As surely as in the unfailing turning of the seasons the earth puts forth growth, so Yahweh will make his righteousness (understood here not only as a moral quality but as vindication as well) grow. Nature, God, and humanity are thus bound together in a mighty life-giving act of recreation and renewal. Messianic glory springs from the earth with human beings (cf. Genesis 2) and by human beings (cf. Second Lesson). In several parts of the world this day has been associated with nature festivals and with the first fruits of the harvest.

The Roman Catholic lesson, from Revelation 11–12, reveals a mystical theophany which centers on a pregnant woman clothed with the sun, with the moon under her feet and a crown of stars. She seems to represent God's people, both Israel as mother of the Messiah and the church the bride of the Lamb. There is a dragon too, representing Satan, waiting to devour her child when it is born, but the child is protected by God and the woman also is sustained by him.

In later Christian tradition Mary came to fulfill the role of the woman described in the Apocalypse, but the preacher should avoid making the identification of this queen of heaven with Mary too explicit. The author of Revelation seemed not to have had Mary in mind in the passage but rather the prevalent myths of the birth of a divine child from a celestial mother.

The **Second Lesson** is the only mention outside of the Gospels and Acts (1:14) of Jesus' mother, and it sets this commemoration of Mary in its proper context: she is the mother of the Lord. (Paul seems unaware of the virginal conception.)

In Galatians, Paul is discussing the role of the law. Although the law could not make people righteous, it showed people God's will so that they might recognize their sin. It was given, not directly from God himself but by angels as mediators, as an addition to the covenant with Abraham because of sin, and it was to function as a custodian until Christ came. At the beginning of chap. 4, Paul uses another illustration of the role of the law. A minor child, although potentially a lord, is subject to guardians and property managers who direct his affairs and his very life until he comes of age. During this period, the minor is no different from a servant. So humankind has been under the direction of the law.

But now, Paul proclaims, the day of majority has arrived. The fullness of time, long prepared by God, has come. History has a purpose, providence has been at work all the while, and at last everything was ready. The pre-existing Son was sent by God into the conditions of human life as a minor subject to the same legal control all people know. He was sent to set free those who had been subject to the law, so we (notice Paul's shift in pronoun) might be adopted as children and be made heirs at last (cf. Jesus' own prayer, Our Father). He shared our condition so we could share his.

The preacher here especially must guard against the easily-made sexist nouns and pronouns as the address becomes yet more personal. Paul speaks directly to the Galatians, "You are sons" to whom God has given his Spirit by which you are enabled to cry "Abba," "Daddy," (cf. Mark 14:36; Rom. 8:15). Finally Paul's address moves to the singular. "You (thou) are no more a slave but a son and if a son then an heir." Maturity has come, and with it has come liberation.

The Roman Catholic lesson, 1 Cor. 15:20–26, also sets this festival on a firm christological foundation and puts it in the context of Easter. Christ is "the first fruits of those who have fallen asleep" (cf. the old name for this festival, the Dormition or the Falling Asleep of the Virgin Mary). The Passover was at least in part a festival of the beginning of the barley harvest (cf. Lev. 23:10–11). As the first fruits were a sign of the harvest to come, so the resurrection of Jesus is a promise of the resurrection of his people which is to come.

The *Gospel* is the song of Mary (a few manuscripts ascribe it to Elizabeth) setting forth the character of God. It has been sung daily by the church at vespers since very ancient times. Mary's song is the church's song of liberation and of revolution, based on the song put into Hannah's mouth at the birth of Samuel (1 Sam. 2:1–10). The song is less a review of Hebrew history testifying to God's acts in the past than a confident assertion of the certainty that God's word now spoken is as good as fulfilled (cf. First Lesson; Gen. 1:3; Isa. 55:11). So the church, aware of continued injustice and hunger, can sing the song with confidence nonetheless, looking toward the final fulfillment of the promise in the eschatological age, begun now but not yet completed. The song tells of the great reversals of salvation history, comfort to the oppressed but a warning to the oppressor.

The song moves from the personal experience of God's goodness (vv. 46–49) to a consideration of God as savior of Israel from her proud oppressors (vv. 50–55). Personal and national concerns merge, and Mary's experience is but an example, although the principal one, of God's revolutionary care—moral, social, economic.

St. Bartholomew, Apostle

AUGUST 24

Lutheran	*Roman Catholic*	*Episcopal*
Exod. 19:1–6*		Deut. 18:15–18†
1 Cor. 12:27–31a‡	Rev. 21:9b–14§	1 Cor. 4:9–15
John 1:43–51‖	John 1:45–51‖	Luke 22:24–30

Bartholomew, a patronymic meaning "son of Tolmai," suggests that this Apostle may have had another, personal name. Nathaniel has been suggested (cf. John 1:45–51; 21:2), since "Bartholomew" is mentioned only in the synoptics and Acts, and Nathaniel of Cana is mentioned only in John. Beyond the name, nothing further is known about him. According to tradition he was martyred by being flayed alive in Armenia where he was a missionary. He is pictured in a prominent place in the Sistine Chapel in Michelangelo's fresco of the Last Judgment.

The general theme of the gift of God helps tie the readings of this feast together. In the *First Lesson* Yahweh makes a covenant with his people, binding them to him forever. The parties to the covenant are not equal, and Yahweh is not as dependent upon Israel as they are upon him. He remains free and sovereign (Deuteronomy 6). This solemn agreement involves a promise made by God, and this mystery of divine choice requires a free acceptance on the part of the people.

Yahweh concluded a covenant with Noah that involved the whole human race (Gen. 9:9). The covenant made with Abraham involved God and an individual patriarch and so was renewed with Jacob (Gen. 28:10 ff.). It required but one obligation: circumcision. The covenant made on Sinai binds the whole nation and the whole nation receives a code of conduct which functions as instruction in the proper life and as a deterrent against transgression which cancels the promise and invites judgment. Sinai (called Horeb, the Mount of God in the Elohistic tradition) stands as the symbol of the law and the place of primary revelation where God called Moses to his service (Exod. 3:1 ff.) and where God and Moses conversed (cf. Gal. 4:24 f.). So the exodus and the passage of the Red Sea were a preliminary promise as God brought Israel to himself (Sinai).

The earth belongs to God who can choose from it any nation to be his, and in his free grace he chooses Israel to be his own special possession, peculiarly his alone. The nation is to have the status and responsibility of priests, mediating between God and humankind and to represent the world to God and to show him to the nations. They are to share in the holiness of God which is at once a gift and a duty. They are witnesses to the interaction between God and his people and are to participate in the communication. The law is a mediator between God and the world, for humankind cannot look directly at God and direct revelation would destroy.

The Episcopal lesson, Deut. 18:15–18, follows a condemnation of superstition, magic, and divination. Instead of these, God will raise up for his people another prophet (probably to be understood as a singular collective, suggesting a succession of prophets) like Moses, the prototype of a prophet and spokesman for God. He will be the mediator and representative of God to the people. The passage gave rise to expectations of a messianic second Moses (cf. Acts 3:22; 7:37; and the Gospel, Philip's description of Jesus as "him of whom Moses in the law . . . wrote"). His task was to mediate God—his presence, words, authority—to Israel, and prophecy is the means in the kingdom of mediation between God and people.

The **Second Lesson** is a statement of the variety of gifts given to the Christian church—a rich diversity within unity. The movement is from the one to the many and not *vice versa* and insists not on the rights of the many but on their duties. Everyone has his gift, yet not all have the same service to perform.

The order of the offices seems to indicate what Paul considers to be their rank. The apostles are first—not only the twelve but other eyewitnesses of Jesus also who were "sent out" to proclaim what they had seen and known (Acts 1:22). Instead of a book or written law, Jesus, when the days of his earthly ministry were concluded, left men and women who had been with him.

The apostles were eyewitnesses to Christ. The prophets were witnesses to the Spirit: NT people who had experienced a renewed outpouring of the Spirit that had been sealed since the close of the OT prophetic age. They lived close to the presence of God and knew his mind and heart and will and revealed them to the church in judgment and in guidance. They edified the church by supernatural revelation.

The teachers are the third order, charged with the slower, more patient building of the church by instructing the converts in their faith. They open up the secrets and the treasure of the church not by ecstasy but with patient labor, reminding their students of things they did not know they knew (cf. Acts 13:1).

Social workers follow: workers of miracles, healers, helpers (i.e., those who gave to works of charity, who ministered to physical health). These offices seem to be among those later gathered into the responsibility of the deacons.

The administrators are yet further subordinated, as essential as this work is. They may be the bishops or overseers Paul speaks of in Phil. 1:1. Finally there are speakers in tongues, listed last by Paul because of their often unintelligible languages, which Paul argues (1 Cor. 14:5) are of dubious value without an interpreter. Nonetheless the gift of tongues is a gift of the Spirit, a continuation of Pentecost and the ecstatic states associated with prophecy in the OT.

Finally, Paul warns that each must earnestly desire not the gifts that are noticeable but those which are "higher" and work for the good of the community, developing whatever gifts one has. The best way of all is the way of love (chap. 13).

The Episcopal lesson is 1 Cor. 4:9–15, in which Paul sarcastically addresses the self-satisfied Corinthians on the smugness that reveals spiritual poverty. He suggests that the apostles might be ranked not first but last, sentenced to death, having no qualities the world would honor or respect. Such, he implies, is the calling not only of apostles but of the whole church when it gets beyond self-satisfied pride and contentment with the status quo.

The Roman Catholic lesson is the account of John the Divine's vision of the New Jerusalem with twelve gates for the twelve tribes of Israel and resting upon twelve foundation stones of the twelve Apostles (Eph. 2:20). It is a general passage emphasizing the importance of the old Israel and the new in the messianic kingdom and the role of the Apostles in the city of the consummation. Without them and without their witness, there would be no church.

The selection of John 1:43–51 as the *Gospel* for St. Bartholomew's Day assumes that Nathaniel is to be identified with Bartholomew. The earliest suggestions, however, are that he is not one of the twelve, and not all critics accept the identification. Without stressing this identification, the preacher can nonetheless use the text as illustrative of the general theme of the day's readings—the gift of God ("Nathaniel" means "God has given"). He symbolically shows Israel coming to God.

Andrew and another are called by Jesus to be disciples. Andrew brings his brother, Simon Peter, to Jesus. Philip (from the same town as Andrew and Peter) is summoned by Jesus, and Philip brings Nathaniel to Jesus, who welcomes him as a true Israelite.

The narrative moves from Philip's description of Jesus to Nathaniel ("him of whom the prophets wrote, Jesus son of Joseph"; cf. the Episcopal Second Lesson) to Nathaniel's confession after his initial skepticism (there was no OT prophecy about Nazareth), "You are the Son of God! You are the king of Israel!" to Jesus' prediction of still greater insight. Nathaniel's greatness is his willingness to "come and see"; (cf. 9:29, 41). Unlike the other Jews, the true Israelite believes in Jesus, the Fourth Gospel implies, and so Nathaniel is the real representative of Israel (cf. 1:11–13).

Jacob, whose name was also Israel (Gen. 32:28–30) was a man of guile and deceit (e.g., Gen. 27:35). Moreover, it was popularly thought that the name Israel meant "seeing God" as Jacob saw God "face to face" (Gen. 32:27–30). So Jesus promises Nathaniel, "You shall see greater things than these" (cf. v. 51; Gen. 28:12). The reference seems to be to the unique mediatorship of Jesus in whom heaven and earth meet, who always, but especially on the last day, unites God and man. Nathaniel's title for Jesus, "Son of God," seems to be a messianic assertion (Ps. 2:6–7), for Jesus saw Nathaniel under a fig tree which may suggest Mic. 4:4, which pictures each man sitting under his fig tree in the messianic kingdom. Moreover, "Son of God" not only climaxes the progression of titles given to Jesus in this opening chapter of the Fourth Gospel, but foreshadows Thomas' confession of Jesus' divinity in chap. 20, "My Lord and my God."

The Episcopal Gospel, the traditional one for St. Bartholomew's Day, is the dispute about greatness in the kingdom that broke out at the Last Supper. This Gospel avoids the Bartholomew-Nathaniel equation and instead, in what seems to be a very ancient saying echoing the sound of Jesus' speech distinctly, emphasizes the glory of the twelve, who, having shared the trials of Jesus, will share the messianic banquet with him (as they now have shared the Supper) and sit on thrones judging or ruling the twelve tribes (of Israel and the church). The kingdom, promised by the Father to Jesus, is in turn promised by Jesus to the Apostles.

Holy Cross Day

SEPTEMBER 14

Lutheran	*Roman Catholic*	*Episcopal*
Isa. 45:21–25*	Num. 21:4–9†	Isa. 45:21–25*
1 Cor. 1:18–24‡	Phil. 2:6–11§	Phil. 2:5–11§
John 12:20–33#	John 3:13–17**	or Gal. 6:14–18‖
		John 12:31–36#

Christian piety and devotion rather naturally were attached to the instrument by which the world's salvation was won. Made holy by its use, washed with Christ's blood, the cross on which Jesus died was early surrounded with honor. It was personified and addressed by poetic apostrophe, seen as jeweled and resplendent. As Jesus was the second Adam, the cross was the second tree, replacing with life the tree of death in the garden. The liturgy almost always views the cross as a sign of triumph (so the present Roman Catholic name for the day is "The Triumph of the

* see Christmas 1, Series B
† see Lent 4, Series B
‡ see Tuesday of Holy Week, Series A, B, and C
§ see Pentecost 19, Series A; Sunday of the Passion, Series A, B, and C
‖ see Pentecost 7, Series C
\# see Lent 5, Series B; Tuesday of Holy Week, Series A, B, and C
** see Holy Trinity, Series B; Lent 4, Series B

Cross") rather than as an instrument of torture. Two of the great hymns of the Christian tradition were written in honor of the cross: *Pange lingua gloriosi* ("Sing my tongue the glorious battle") and *Vexilla regis prodeunt* ("The royal banners forward go").

The choice of this day as Holy Cross Day is a rather curious story. Cyril of Jerusalem (d. 386) says that the cross was found in the time of Constantine; this discovery of what was thought to be the actual instrument of crucifixion was perhaps made during excavations for a basilica (dedicated in 335) which Constantine erected on the supposed site of the Holy Sepulchre. The Spanish pilgrim Etheria, who travelled to Jerusalem ca. 385–388, mentions the adoration of the cross there but gives no date for the veneration. In 614 the supposed true cross fell into the hands of the Persians. The emperor Heraclius recovered it and put it on view at Jerusalem in the spring of 629. Holy Cross Day has its origins as a commemoration of that event but moved to the day in the fall that was associated with the finding of the cross in Jerusalem. There has been some shifting between May 3 and September 14 as the proper date for the observance through the centuries.

Moreover, Holy Cross Day marked the autumnal Ember Days. These were seasons of prayer associated with the agricultural cycle: sowing in Advent, the grain harvest following Pentecost, and the wine harvest in September. Later the first week of Lent was added to give a liturgical recognition to the turning of each of the four seasons.

A basic theme for this day is the universality of God's purpose. The *First Lesson* is part of an oracle telling of the conversion of the nations to monotheism. The survivors of the nations (that is, those who have escaped judgment—cf. 66:19) are gathered as at a judicial proceeding. Those who have survived the crisis of the changing world order are challenged to confess that Yahweh was preparing this moment of salvation "from the beginning" and to present their case (v. 21) which will be shown to have no merit for their god is a powerless idol which cannot save nor help. They carried their god in procession (religious processions seen in Babylon shape the image); Yahweh, in contrast, carried his people (40:11; 46:3). All who raged and warred against Yahweh will come to him ashamed and overcome by his great strength. No illness nor unhappiness dare stain the glory of the eschatological kingdom. Yahweh has foreseen it and told of it long ago, for he has absolute control, and he alone can deliver and give victory.

He has bound himself by an oath (Gen. 22:16; Exod. 32:13; Amos 6:8; Jer. 22:5; Heb. 6:13–18) and has spoken his word, which is filled with divine energy and power and which is even now at work in the world fulfilling what it was spoken to accomplish (55:11). The hiddenness of God himself to the nations is contrasted with the openness of his word. Every individual in all the nations will worship God alone, and all idolatry will be ended (cf. Phil. 2:10–11; Rom. 14:11). The new age is about to begin, and the sweep of the messianic hope is exhilarating. Even rebellion is tamed to his purpose (and the cross becomes the instrument of the world's salvation).

The conclusion is therefore a summons to the nations to accept the salvation which is offered. There is but one requirement: return to God in humble faith. God's redemptive activity has gone forth and the proclamation of the line of prophets bears witness to it and participates in it. So the nations stream to worship Yahweh (cf. Mic. 4:1–4), and the progeny of Israel are beyond number, a vast throng. The whole world will belong to the chosen people. This grand vision of universal worship is echoed in Phil. 2:10 ff., the universal worship of the glorified Christ. "I, if I be lifted up from the earth, will draw all men to me."

The Roman Catholic lesson, Num. 21:4–9, tells of the bronze serpent Moses made and set on a pole as an antidote to the attack of poisonous snakes (their bite caused an inflammation apparently), which were understood to be a divine judgment on the people's rebellion. The background to the event lies in serpent magic—the cult of snakes was widespread in Canaan—(cf. 2 Kings 18:4), but the event was seen by Jesus as a prototype of himself (John 3:14). By faith in the one on the tree, the repentant sinner would be healed and live (cf. 1 Cor. 10:9).

God's power to save, which the First Lesson declares, is made known, according to the Christian gospel, in a paradoxical way: the cross. The *Second Lesson*, therefore, presents the "theology of the cross" as Luther called it, the way of humility, pain, and death as the God-pleasing and the God-chosen way to deliver his people and by which his people are to live. The cross is the democratizing force in the church, for it confounds all human ways of thinking and of ranking its members. Before the cross all are equal, for there they are recipients of a gift. All one's tradition and wisdom and morality are upset and confounded, for human effort can neither comprehend God nor fathom his ways.

The lesson suggests that people need saving even more than they need teaching. The preacher might address himself to America's elevation of education to the level of a religion, as the supposed way to success and power, the one thing worth sacrificing for. The benefits of wisdom are enormous, but, the lesson reminds us, they cannot save nor necessarily lead to God. The preacher who chooses this approach must beware of glorifying ignorance. Thomas Aquinas observed that people tend to regard as foolishness whatever is beyond their understanding.

Wisdom for the Jew is found in the law. Wisdom for the Greek is found in philosophy. But both, Paul says, are the wisdom of the world, that which is unredeemed and under the power of Satan (1 Cor. 2:6; 2 Cor. 4:4). Holy Wisdom is the Spirit who enlightens and teaches the church to see the wisdom of God dying on a cross. And that shatters (Jewish) nationalism and (Greek) intellectualism. Contrary to the expectations of many Jews of the time, God's wisdom has no signs of power and domination of the Gentiles. Humility and service remain. Contrary to the expectations of the Greeks, the cross is no large, coherent, systematic explanation of humanity and the cosmos. The mystery remains. And the church stands still in contemplation before the crucifix with the inscription "You were bought with a price" (1 Cor. 6:20).

The cross upsets all ordinary understanding, all common sense. It is the voluntary assumption of pain and suffering by God and so by his people, when one does not need to do it and when no one would think any less of one for avoiding it. What would have been more sensible and moral than for God to have abandoned a wicked and rebellious world headed for destruction?

The Roman Catholic and Episcopal reading is from Philippians 2, the hymn on humiliation and exaltation. Because of Jesus' willing renunciation of the glory that was rightfully and eternally his, God exalted him to unparalleled heights so that all creation could acknowledge him as sovereign Lord. (As William Penn put it, "No cross, no crown.") What has been accomplished now will be acknowledged at the parousia, and at last the goal of creation and redemption will be achieved.

The Episcopal alternate reading is Gal. 6:14–18—glorying in the cross of Jesus Christ. The cross here is the whole "Christ-event" and the "world" which it crucifies is all that is opposed to God and his will, all pleasure and ambition. Paul died, as do all Christians, not by a private mystical experience (though this may also occur, as it did with Paul), but by the historical event of the crucifixion. It is nothing less than a new shaping of existence through the life-giving Spirit of Christ. But this new creation will still bear the marks of suffering (cf. the glorified Jesus, John 20:27), which in the followers of Jesus are the brands of new ownership.

In the *Gospel* some Greek proselytes (but cf. Acts 8:27) representing the Gentile world come to Jesus, and with their approach Jesus has no further dealings with Israel alone. The transition to the universality spoken of in the First Lesson and which the death and resurrection of Jesus are to accomplish has begun. The arrival of the Gentiles indicates that "The hour has come" (v. 23). They come to "see" Jesus, wanting to talk with him. What they were soon to see with the deepening sight of faith is the glorification of Jesus in death and resurrection (cf. 1:50–51; 20:29). These Greeks are never described as actually meeting Jesus: the world-wide mission which they represent is dependent upon his death and resurrection.

Jesus teaches the archetypal mystery of death and life which has fascinated humankind since the ancient planting societies drew parallels between their crops and themselves. Death is necessary for life. The seed must be buried to make it grow; death is the life of the living (cf. the Ember Days' agricultural associations). So Jesus must die to bring larger life and so must his disciples share with him his death and resurrection. But the dying and rising of which Jesus speaks is a decisive once and for all event, chosen deliberately by Jesus. Such total selflessness and absolute willingness to offer one's life must characterize each believer. The way to life is through the renunciation of life.

This inclusive view of the work Jesus came to do sees not tragedy followed by triumph but rather sees the two inextricably mixed, with the triumph always present, even—especially—at the moment of death ("It is consummated!"). It involves struggle, testing, and trying the obedience of the Son to the Father and later of the children to the Son and the Father. Jesus here and his disciples after him confront the awful reality of existence requiring death and life. The voice from heaven confirms the unity of what Jesus has done in his ministry and what he will do in his death and resurrection. Both are manifestations of divine glory and triumph. So he can speak imprecisely about being "lifted up" (cf. Isa. 52:13; John 3:14–15—the Roman Catholic Gospel; John 8:28) suggesting both the elevation on the cross in death and the elevation to heaven in glory. The editorial comment, "He said this to show by what death he was to die," is equally ambiguous: the manner of death, i.e., crucifixion (in which Jesus' arms were stretched out in invitation to all), and also the kind of death, i.e., one that leads to life for himself and his people. When that one event takes place, he will fulfill the universalistic vision of the prophets and draw all humanity to himself.

Darkness is about to descend. Jesus will go away into death, and then soon after leave off all earthly appearances. The reading, as lengthened in the Episcopal lectionary, urges people to believe in him before it is too late. Then they can become the children of light (1:4–5, 12–13; 8:12; Isa. 49:5–6) and share his life which is life in its fullness and maturity.

Such was the intent of the voice from heaven, and such was God's intention from the beginning. With urgent insistence, the evangelist emphasizes the current crisis and the opportunity for faith: *"Now* is my soul troubled. . . . *Now* is the judgment of this world." The old creation is ending; the new is beginning. With this challenge and urgent appeal (cf. Mark 13:35–37) his public ministry has reached its conclusion. After this, in John's Gospel, Jesus no longer speaks publicly.

St. Matthew, Apostle and Evangelist

SEPTEMBER 21

Lutheran	*Roman Catholic*	*Episcopal*
Ezek. 2 :8–3 :11		Prov. 3 :1–6
Eph. 2 :4–10*	Eph. 4 :1–7, 11–13†	2 Tim. 3 :14–17‡
Matt. 9 :9–13§	Matt. 9 :9–13§	Matt. 9 :9–13§

This day is one of the most ancient commemorations in the calendar. A mass was appointed for it in the martyrology of St. Jerome. Matthew (according to Mark, the son of Alphaeus) was a tax collector in Capernaum, called from his desk by Jesus to be an Apostle. The Gospels of Mark (2:14) and Luke (5:27) call him Levi, which may have been his original name, Matthew (meaning in Hebrew "gift from God") perhaps having been given to him after he became a disciple; or "Levi" may mean "the Levite." Since the second century the first Gospel has been attributed to him. Nothing further is known about him. In art, Matthew is represented by a winged man (suggested by Ezek. 1:1–10 and 10:8–14). In the East, his feast day is November 16. The day is a good occasion for a congregation to examine the character, structure, and point of view of Matthew's Gospel: written for the Jews, emphasizing Jesus' teaching, with a strong apocalyptic interest. The precise relationship between Matthew the Apostle and the Gospel as it now stands is uncertain.

* see Lent 4, Series B
† see Pentecost 10, Series B
‡ see Pentecost 22, Series C
§ see Pentecost 3, Series A

The *First Lesson* records the commission of the prophet who received his call by a vision of the scroll. (The call of Ezekiel involves five different commissions.) Ezekiel, like the other prophets, was given a message of impending divine judgment (cf. Amos 8:1–3; Isa. 6:11–13; Jer. 1:13–19): "lamentation and mourning and woe" were inscribed not as usual on one side only but on the front and the back, so all-pervading was the approaching doom. Ezekiel makes vivid his charge to proclaim the word: he is to eat the book ("digest it" we still say in a dead metaphor). Ezekiel is to appropriate to himself the contents, to identify with them and totally assimilate the message. It is a graphic representation of an inner experience which was not entirely subjective. Isaiah's mouth was touched by the seraph (Isa. 6:5–7) to cleanse and empower him. Yahweh himself put his words into Jeremiah's mouth (Jer. 1:9). Although Ezekiel sees only a hand, his image is more striking still, and the reader learns even of the taste of the scroll; for all its lamentation, it was as "sweet as honey" (cf. Ps. 19:10; 119:103; Exod. 16:31; Rev. 10:4–10). The words, for all their woeful import, were divine and therefore pleasant to taste.

The unwelcome message will meet stubborn opposition, but the prophet is commanded and empowered by God to be determined to prophesy despite Israel's refusal to hear (cf. John 1:11). The connection with Matthew's Gospel is clear: Matthew is addressed to the Jews to show Jesus as the promised Messiah. The Gospel moreover is aware of the problem of unbelief—the majority of Jews did not believe in Jesus. Resistance is strongest and most adamant within the people of God. Outsiders, the Gentiles, are ready to hear, but Israel (the church) refuses. The problem is always not to convert the world but to convert (Israel) the church. Belief is a gift from God (13:11; 16:17) that remains a mystery that cannot be dispelled: some believe and some do not.

The Episcopal lesson, Prov. 3:1–6, is a general admonition to faithful adherence to the life-giving commands of God, binding them on externally and digesting them internally in the heart. Reliance upon Yahweh and not upon oneself will result in his guidance. The "commandments" of God recall Matthew's emphasis on the law and his picture of Jesus, like Moses on Sinai, delivering the Sermon on the Mount. Kindness and fidelity (vv. 3–4) are the qualities that characterize the God of the Sinai covenant in his relationship with Israel and which should characterize Israel's relationship to God and neighbors. The key phrase of the reading is perhaps "do not forget," which depends upon the biblical understanding of "remember" in the sense of keeping alive in the memory, keeping present the formative events by which the nation of Israel and the church were made.

The *Second Lesson* is a Pauline answer to a problem raised by Matthew's Gospel, particularly for evangelical Christians: the role of good works, of rewards and punishments. The reading from Ephesians 2 makes clear that redemption is wholly the gift of God. It is a theme that needs constant emphasis, for it is a theme that is seldom understood in the life of the people of God. Nothing we do can earn God's favor; his goodness to his people is due entirely to his gracious nature (v. 8).

The widespread, pervasive, and continuing ignorance of this doctrine of the primacy of grace is no doubt due to shallow devotional lives. Those like Paul, with the most to boast of, are the least willing to claim God's attention and are instead awed by his choice of them and his continued graciousness to them. When the Christian becomes aware of all that God has done for his people—giving him who was dead life and raising him to sit in heavenly places with Christ (vv. 5–6)—no work or deed or quality of life can compare with such an overwhelming gift. We are set where God is with his power and salvation, honor and authority. The task of the preacher, therefore, is so to proclaim the richness of what God in his goodness has done that the response is gratitude and a new desire to reshape one's life in accordance with the divine directives (v. 10). We are recreated and reformed for service. Undeserving, we nevertheless receive love, and that gift has its effect in us—a new joy and a new freedom in serving not ourselves and not simply God but the world.

The Roman Catholic lesson, also from Ephesians, the epistle of Christian unity, is the beginning of a selection on the practical application of the previous doctrine. Those who are called to share in the great mystery must live worthy of their calling. The Spirit, continually moving in all the members to promote harmony and peace, is the inner source of Christian life. The reading is an appeal to maintain unity, which consists of seven elements: one body, spirit, hope, Lord, faith, baptism, Father. Within that seven-fold unity is found a variety of gifts, each for the building up of the community toward maturity. So among these ministers of the word, Matthew's gift was to be an evangelist. The Christian is urged to discover and use his or her gift also in order to help build the church.

The Episcopal lesson, 2 Tim. 3:14–17, speaks of the inspiration of the entirety of Scripture, i.e., the OT, into which God has breathed his Spirit ("in-spired"); cf. Gen. 2:7. The authority of the Bible is rooted in the authority of God who is ultimately responsible for these books. Timothy is admonished here to remain in the tradition in which he has been brought up (his teachers were his mother and grandmother—1:5—and Paul—vv. 10–11), for it points to faith in Christ. Such was the message of Matthew, "that it might be fulfilled which was spoken by the prophet. . . ."

The **Gospel** moves from controversy to a saying. The identification of the author of the Gospel with Matthew the tax collector is "almost certainly a fiction"; the Gospel itself does not make the claim. Perhaps Matthew made a collection of Jesus' sayings (as a tax gatherer and one who was used to keeping records might be expected to do naturally) that was used by the anonymous Christian teacher who prepared the Gospel in the last quarter of the first century.

Matthew's Gospel has made Mark's account of the call of Matthew more consistent. Mark has Jesus call "Levi" from his tax desk but lists "Matthew" as one of the twelve; in Matthew's Gospel, however, the call is understood as the choice of one of the twelve. Whatever Matthew knew of Jesus before is incidental. The point—as with the call of Andrew (4:18–22)—is that pattern of the call of Abraham. A man is summoned to leave the security of a comfortable and well-paying job and to embark on a perilous and unknown journey. (Matthew's ready acceptance of the call is the more remarkable since he was so unlikely a prospect.) As Eric Milner-White's collect prays, "O Lord God, who hast called thy servants to ventures of which we cannot see the ending, by paths as yet untrodden, through perils unknown; give us faith to go out with a good courage, not knowing whither we go, but only that thy hand is leading us and thy love supporting us; to the glory of thy name." From security to glory, from greed to service, from selfishness to selflessness, from gathering to giving —the contrast between old and new could not be more plain.

Tax-gatherers were despised by the Jews as traitors, for they were in the service of the oppressor and were usually unscrupulous besides, amassing fortunes from the misfortune of their country. They could not enter the synagogue, and they were classed with the unclean beasts. Jesus' call of Matthew was no token gesture but a clear evidence of his commitment to the outcast. He welcomed the unwelcome to his table in the face of the Pharisees' demand for ritual purity, adherence to the law, and separation from all that was unworthy. It is not clear from Matthew or Mark whose house the dinner was held in, although Luke says it was Levi's. The ambiguity perhaps suggests that no matter whose house it was, Jesus was the host, the one clearly in charge (v. 13).

Jesus recognizes that his opponents were in some sense acceptable to God, and he pleads for a place for the despised and the excluded. The demand of the new law is mercy, not sacrifice (Hos. 6:6). This was also the heart of the old law as the prophets made clear (Isa. 1:10–20; 58: 6–12; Mic. 6:8), inner commitment and attitude, not external concern. The meal that Jesus shares with the outcasts points to the eschatological feast which is likewise an inclusive banquet. The point, then, is God's shocking and overwhelming generosity.

St. Michael and All Angels

SEPTEMBER 29

Lutheran	*Roman Catholic*	*Episcopal*
Dan. 10:10–14 ; 12:1–3	Dan. 7:9–10, 13–14*	Gen. 28:10–17†
Rev. 12:7–12	or Rev. 12:7–12a	Rev. 12:7–11
Luke 10:17–20	John 1:47–51‡	John 1:47–51‡

Michael the archangel, the guardian of the people of God, has been held in honor since before the beginning of Christianity, for he is venerated also by the Jews. He is mentioned four times in Scripture: Dan. 10:13; 12:1; Jude 9; and Rev. 12:7–9. According to Revelation 12, Michael, whose name has been thought to mean "who is like God," led the heavenly army against Lucifer and the rebellious angels. It is therefore Michael and not God who is the counterpart of Satan (cf. Jude 9). An ancient tradition holds that it is Michael who receives the souls of the dead. He was once honored as a healer and was associated with hot water springs in Greece and Asia.

This festival in his honor has its origins in the dedication to Michael of a small basilica near Rome in the fifth century. In the new Roman Catholic calendar, the archangels Michael, Gabriel, and Raphael are commemorated together on this day. The churches of the Reformation have regarded it as a feast of all the angels; it is the oldest and originally the only angel festival. An important aspect of the festival for modern times is that it celebrates the unseen dimensions of the universe, whole worlds of beings that are beyond human understanding.

The *First Lesson* is from Daniel's vision of the last days, the time of wrath and the end. Daniel has collapsed in rapture at the sight of a dazzling celestial man (angel?) dressed in linen. The reading opens with a hand of someone (a man? an angel, perhaps Gabriel in a less dazzling form?) raising Daniel somewhat and telling him to stand to hear the word he has been sent to deliver. The message has been sent because of

* see Last Pentecost, Series B   ‡ see Epiphany 2, Series B
† see Lent 2, Series B

the seer's desire to understand the vision. The messenger would have arrived three weeks before, except the patron and guardian angel of Persia (cf. Deut. 32:8) opposed him until Michael in his role as defender came to the messenger's assistance. (Such championing of opposing sides by the angels perhaps indicates that not even they know the secret will of God which is yet to be revealed.) But now the messenger has arrived (v. 14) with his message about events leading up to the end. He brings insight into the meaning of history and suggests the cooperation of Gabriel and Michael in the transition from the Babylonian empire to the Medean.

Apocalyptic writing, such as this, arises to sustain faith and hope in times of distress. By signs and symbols the current crisis is interpreted as being yet under God's control and as issuing at length in triumph and peace. The Book of Daniel was one of the last books of the OT to be written (167–164 B.C. in the reign of Antiochus Epiphanes). The tribulation will become intense as the end approaches, but faith is not to be abandoned, for Michael fights for his people, and the new age is about to begin. The remnant who have been faithful throughout the tribulation will receive their everlasting reward. Not even death will stand in the way of justice; many (meaning all?) will be raised to shame or to life. This is the earliest clear statement in the Bible of belief in the resurrection of the dead.

The Roman Catholic lesson, Dan. 7:9–10, 13–14, is the account of Daniel's vision of God, the Ancient One, sitting in judgment and of a mysterious celestial man, who contrasts with the preceding bestial figures (7:1–8), being presented before him to receive universal and everlasting dominion. This man seems to be an angel who represents the theocratic kingdom of the holy ones of the Most High (v. 18). He is similar to Israel, yet he merges into the angelic host. The man is in heaven near God (Gen. 1–2; Ps. 8:5).

The Episcopal lesson, Gen. 28:10–17, Jacob's vision of the stair set up between heaven and earth, is probably to be understood as a picture inspired by a Mesopotamian ziggurat temple town (cf. v. 17: "the house of God and gate of heaven"). The dream happened at night (theophanies often occur at night in the mystery of darkness) at a Canaanite sanctuary. The basic point of the incident is to show that the God of the patriarchs is not limited spatially and that he has fundamental control over the vagaries of history. The individual is free, but only on the surface, and is part of a larger pattern over which he does not have control. Jacob the fugitive is permitted to glimpse the larger truth. He sees beyond the angels to what they signify: the presence of God who is the God of the patriarchs and not the god of the pagan sanctuary.

The **Second Lesson** records perhaps the strangest event in the entire Bible—war in heaven (cf. Eph. 6:12). Rebellion had broken out even there. According to one tradition, Satan rebelled because he envied God's power ("Better to reign in hell than serve in heaven," Milton has him say); according to another tradition, Satan refused to worship the man God had made and who pleased him so. Michael, the champion of Israel, who is mentioned nowhere else in Revelation, is victorious in the celestial war and the rebellious angels are expelled (cf. Isa. 14:12 ff.; Luke 10:18). The devil ("slanderer") or Satan ("accuser") is thus in temporary control of the world (v. 12).

The struggle is continued on earth as Satan the accuser slanders the servants of God for whom Michael the defender fights. The death of the sacrificial Lamb (1:5) is his victory over Satan, and the martyrs by their deaths participate in the death of the Lamb (cf. John 12:25). So Michael's victory is possible because of the enthronement of the Lamb, and therefore Christians can be sure that they will conquer Satan on earth. The victory is God's and his reign is already established and is celebrated (12:11; 11:15) as a past event—it is that certain. The Lamb is the church's Paraclete before God (cf. 1 John 2:1) removing sin and silencing the accuser. His sacrifice brings victory to those who make themselves victims with him (cf. Rom. 8:17; 2 Tim. 2:11) and choose the path of self-renunciation.

One's understanding is depleted if it is limited merely to what one can see. The angels show dimensions of the universe beyond human understanding and sight, and the struggle they engage in suggests the battle between the individual, supported by Michael and his host, and the organized forces of supernatural evil beings (Rom. 8:38).

The **Gospel:** It is not clear from Revelation when the war in heaven was understood to have taken place. Some traditions place it before the beginning of history, some before the reign of the Messiah. Similarly, Jesus saying in the Gospel, "I saw Satan fall like lightning" (cf. Isa. 14:12) can be understood as a reference to Jesus' pre-existence or to a vision he had, while the seventy were doing their ministry, of the fall of Satan which happened then or which was to take place sometime in the future. The victory is probably best understood as a continuing experience as evil yields before the march of good as the new age advances. The kingdom of God is breaking the power of Satan who is already defeated. The effects of that victory are to be felt in the church and are made real there (cf. Ps. 91:13; Acts 28:6; John 12:31).

The seventy are astonished at the success of their ministry, but Jesus turns them from such joy in their new-found power lest it degenerate into self-congratulation, and he points them toward the only source of joy: not in possessing but in being possessed. Satan, he reminds them, fell from heaven because of pride. The point is not what a person has done, but what God has done for the person.

The earthly success of the seventy was only temporary. The passion had not yet begun. Jesus seems to be warning them against assuming success on the basis of insufficient evidence. That sort of euphoria easily evaporates. Success comes and goes but the one thing that is constant is the election and choice by God. That cannot change.

The Roman Catholic and Episcopal Gospel, John 1:47–51, is used in the Lutheran lectionary on St. Bartholomew's Day. Jesus promises the new disciples that they will see what Jacob saw (Gen. 28:10–17, the Episcopal First Lesson), now made a reality with Jesus as the focal point of heaven and earth, the mediator. Jesus himself is the staircase, the ladder; he is the embodiment of salvation, the one human being who lives with the glory of God. He unites God and his people. He is the abode of God and the gate of heaven. This meeting and communication of God and his people originally probably referred to the resurrection or the parousia. It will come on the last day, but to the eye of faith it is always present.

St. Luke, Evangelist

OCTOBER 18

Lutheran	*Roman Catholic*	*Episcopal*
Isa. 43:8–13 or Isa. 35:5–8*		Ecclus. 38:1–4, 6–10,
2 Tim. 4:5–11†	2 Tim. 4:9–17a†	12–14
Luke 1:1–4; 24:44–53‡	Luke 10:1–9§	2 Tim. 4:5–13†
		Luke 4:14–21‖

Luke was a Gentile physician (Col. 4:14) who was a companion of Paul, perhaps his own physician. The "we" portions of Acts are presumably from his first-hand account (Acts 16:10–17; 20:5–21:18; 27:1–28:6). Luke has been identified with "the brother" of 2 Cor. 8:18 "who

* see Pentecost 16, Series B
† see Pentecost 23, Series B
‡ see Ascension, Series A, B, and C
§ see Pentecost 10, Series C
‖ see Epiphany 3, Series C

is famous among all the churches for his preaching of the gospel"; so the collect for St. Luke's Day in the English *Book of Common Prayer* and in the *Service Book and Hymnal* begins "Almighty God, who didst call Saint Luke the physician, whose praise is in the gospel, to be an evangelist. . . ." There seems to be no convincing reason to doubt the attribution, dating from the second century, of the Third Gospel and the Book of Acts to him, especially since it goes counter to the tendency to ascribe NT writings to the Apostles. Nothing further is known of his life and work, but traditions about him abound: he was born in Antioch, he was one of the seventy sent out by Jesus, he was the other disciple with Cleopas on the road to Emmaus Easter evening, he was a painter who painted a portrait of the Virgin Mary, he died unmarried at the age of eighty-four in Boethia. Both the Eastern and the Western churches commemorate him on October 18. He is traditionally symbolized by a winged ox, as suggested by Ezek. 1:1–10 and 10:8–14.

Luke's Gospel is characterized by universalism, interest in social relationships, a concern for the outcasts, a concern for women, the emphasis on joy and on the Holy Spirit, the emphasis on the graciousness and the lordship of Christ, the interest in the parousia.

The *First Lesson:* The scene is a courtroom (cf. 41:1). Yahweh calls up his people as his witnesses through whom he will confront the nations. Although Israel is blind and deaf, it has the capacity for vision and hearing. It is yet able to be enlightened and be converted. Only Israel of all the nations of the world has a right understanding of the meaning of history. No other nation can match Israel's prophetic tradition, and despite the present blindness and deafness, the Israelites have been witnesses to great events in the past, and their continued existence remains a witness to those formative acts of divine intervention, even though the meaning is largely lost in the present generation (42:20). A silent and unseeing church is made to see and speak and act and explore again the treasure of its tradition. Their eyes have seen and their ears have heard the events, and they were therefore the custodians of that tradition maintained in the narratives of the books of the law and renewed in the oracles of the prophets. The nations are challenged to match that tradition and so prove the validity of their tradition and the existence of their gods. But, the text implies, by their silence, they cannot.

Monotheism is asserted with vigor. There were no gods before Yahweh and there will be no gods after him. He is the only God (the language recalls the covenant): "Besides me there is no savior" (cf. 43:1–3). Israel is to be the servant of God and the prophet who announces this to the nations, fulfilling God's purposes and doing his will. By such service, Israel, although as yet blind to its own tradition and deaf to its own message, will come to knowledge and insight and learn the monotheism it proclaims. Such is the task of the evangelist and the teacher: to learn by teaching, to be converted by preaching, and explore more and more the meaning of experience. It is the theme of revelation and response.

The alternate reading from First (pre-exilic) Isaiah looks to the new exodus and the miraculous cures of the exiles' spiritual blindness, deafness, lameness, and dumbness. Life-giving water will be abundant, even in the desert, and God's holy way will go through the land leading to the holy place, Mt. Zion. The connection between this vision of the transformed world and the commemoration of Luke the physician is plain.

The Episcopal lesson from Ecclesiasticus tells how God works through physicians. The text is useful in directing attention to the work of the healing professions and in directing their attention to God who is the ultimate source of life and health. It is appropriate to Luke's role as the patron of doctors. The reading seems to be but self-evident common sense, but it apparently dealt with a contemporary problem, for some thought that consulting a physician showed a lack of confidence in God.

The **Second Lesson** (see St. Mark's Day) begins with advice to Timothy to be restrained, sober in deportment, enduring suffering, doing the work of an evangelist, which in this context is preaching the gospel (cf. Acts 21:8; Eph. 4:11) without restriction to a particular area. In the case of Luke, an evangelist is a writer of a gospel, and the preacher ought to make this clear. In short, Timothy is to fulfill his ministry, make full use of his developing vocation, which was sealed with the laying-on of hands (1:6–7). If he does that, he will naturally be steady, endure suffering, do the work of a preacher of the gospel.

The writer then turns to himself and his own concerns. He is at the end of his ministry, as Timothy is at the beginning of his. (From now on Timothy will be more or less on his own.) The author is about to be poured out in sacrifice, and, having faithfully fulfilled his ministry, is confident of the victor's crown that awaits him and all, including Timothy, who yearn for the appearing of Jesus Christ and the consummation of the ministry of Christ (cf. the approaching Advent).

The tone of the letter changes at v. 9. Paul is concerned now with personal affairs. (If Paul did not write the pastoral letters as some suggest, this section perhaps has been taken from Paul's writing in another context or is perhaps the remnant of a genuine letter from Paul appended here.) Demas (cf. 3 John 12) has deserted Paul; Crescens and Titus have gone away (on some church business one assumes). Only one—Luke—is yet faithful. Earlier, Luke and Demas were together as Paul's fellow-workers (Col. 4:14; Philem. 24), but now Demas has gone and only Luke remains. Timothy is to bring the now forgiven Mark who will be useful in Paul's service, and the text returns to its opening verse urging fulfillment of the gift of the ministry.

In the Episcopal lectionary the lesson extends to include Paul's request for some needed possessions: a cloak (since winter is coming, v. 21), books (papyrus rolls) of some sort, and most of all the parchments (perhaps simply vellum which had nothing yet written on it; it seems unlikely that they would be collections of Scripture or early Christian writings such as a draft of Luke's Gospel).

The Roman Catholic lesson extends to include Paul's warning against one Alexander who had attacked Paul when he was alone: "no one took my part; all deserted me." Paul has been alone before, and now as always, even if all his companions go away, yet the Lord Jesus Christ stands by him and strengthens him to proclaim the word fully. Again we have returned to the starting place and its urging to faithfulness in the ministry.

The saint speaks to us on his feast day. The **Gospel** according to Luke begins with an introduction similar to the formal prefaces characteristic of the Greek historians, using classical vocabulary, rhetoric, and construction. It is one periodic sentence with elaborately interlocking clauses. The literary quality of the Gospel is notable from the outset.

"Many others" have compiled a narrative (notice that this Gospel like the others was not written from scratch). Perhaps this "many" is to be understood as classical hyperbole meaning "several," but Luke also chooses to compile an account, using sources now unknown to us. He avoids Mark's term "gospel" and stresses instead the historical nature of the work.

Luke presents himself as a second generation Christian who was not an eyewitness to Jesus but who followed things closely for some time (cf. Acts 21:8). The gospel, then, is not simply an historical reporting but is an interpretation of what God was doing in Christ. Real religion is always and ever a personal discovery, even if it is rooted in historical events.

The "Theophilus" to whom both this Gospel and Acts are dedicated, may have been a Roman of high rank, as the title "most excellent" suggests, whose faith sought confirmation or whose support Luke sought or who was still a pagan inquiring about the new religion. But "Theophilus" (which means "lover of God" or "beloved of God") might simply be a personification of the reader whom Luke addresses gracefully and with respect.

The conclusion of the Gospel, 24:44–53, added to the preface to the work in the Lutheran lectionary in an interesting experiment, reports the conclusion of Jesus' earthly ministry, opening the minds of the disciples to the Scriptures, which tell of him. The lesson implies that Theophilus (as well as the present day Christian) who has now heard the gospel, is a witness to "these things" so that the news might be proclaimed to all nations. When they could see Jesus no more, the disciples returned to the temple (where the Gospel began) with the surest sign of the presence of God—joy. The Gospel ends where it began, but with a difference. The OT had been given a new interpretation as it had been fulfilled in the presence of the apostolic witnesses, and the unbelief of Zechariah had been replaced with a joyfully obedient belief. Noteworthy too in these concluding verses of the Gospel is the unity of the resurrection and the ascension which seem to have happened on the same day. (The chronology of Acts is different and separates the two events by forty days.) The Spirit at Pentecost gives individual strength and personal union with Christ so that the church becomes the new temple and the new Jerusalem.

The Roman Catholic Gospel, 10:1–9, Jesus' commission of the seventy to prepare for his coming (cf. Exod. 24:1; Num. 11:16; the table of seventy nations in Genesis 10) recalls the tradition that Luke was one of these seventy. (It is unlikely, since Luke does not call himself an eyewitness.) The key verse for St. Luke's Day is v. 9, "heal the sick and say to them, 'The kingdom of God has come near you.'" The kingdom of peace is already present in Jesus, and people must enter it while they have opportunity. The urgency of the present opportunity is stressed. The universal emphasis of Luke is again apparent: the seventy are to go to Samaria during the lifetime of Jesus as the Apostles are to go to the Gentile world after the ascension.

The Episcopal Gospel, 4:14–21, is Jesus' sermon in the synagogue at Nazareth in which he quotes Isaiah 61 and announces that this Scripture has been fulfilled in their hearing—the poor hear good news, the captives are released, the blind see, the oppressed are relieved, and the year of the Lord's favor has come. The passage from Isaiah and Jesus' terse comment on it are an introduction to the whole of Luke-Acts. They announce the mission of Jesus, prepare for the passion, and hint at the mission to the Gentiles.

St. Simon and St. Jude, Apostles
OCTOBER 28

Lutheran	*Roman Catholic*	*Episcopal*
Jer. 26:(1–6), 7–16*		Deut. 32:1–4
1 John 4:1–6†	Eph. 2:19–22‡	Eph. 2:13–22‡
John 14:21–27§	Luke 6:12–16	John 14:21–27§

The two Apostles commemorated today are joined in the apostolic lists in Luke 6:14–16 and Acts 1:13 and in the church's calendar. Simon was a Canaanean, a Zealot (a fierce nationalist). Jude, so called in English to distinguish him from Judas (i.e., Judah) Iscariot, is usually identified with Thaddaeus (Mark 3:18), called Lebbaeus in Matthew (10:3). In Luke 6:16 Judas is said to be "of James"—perhaps the son (brother?) of James the brother of the Lord (Mark 6:3; Matt. 13:55) or James the younger ("the less"); cf. the Epistle of Jude. A tradition says that Simon and Jude preached and were martyred in Persia. As with many in the apostolic company, the names are known (after a fashion), but the details of their ministry are unrecorded. Their position and their labor were fundamental, but the church rejoices more in the power of God who made it so and in the Christ on whom they rest.

The *First Lesson:* In September-October 609 B.C., perhaps on the occasion of the coronation of Jehoiakim (cf. Luther's posting of the Ninety-five Theses in Wittenberg on the eve of All Saints' Day when crowds would be coming to worship), Jeremiah delivered his uncompromisingly political temple sermon on the theme, "What gives people peace and safety?" (A fuller account of the sermon is given in 7:1–15.) Both that account and this summary seem taken from the memoirs of Baruch, Jeremiah's secretary. Obedience is the only protection, the sermon says. If obedience is not rendered, destruction is certain. Shiloh, eighteen miles north of Jerusalem and an ancient and important holy place, was destroyed ca. 1050 B.C., apparently by the Philistines (1 Sam. 4:11), although the Bible does not tell of the destruction of the city or

* see Pentecost 27, Series A; Lent 2, Series C   ‡ see Pentecost 9, Series B
† see Easter 6, Series B   § see Easter 6, Series C

its sanctuary. In Jeremiah's day the ruins were probably still visible, a vivid reminder that not even a holy place was necessarily immune from destruction.

The sermon of course aroused immediate and intense antagonism. If Jeremiah had committed blasphemy, he must die (Exod. 22:28; Lev. 24:10 ff.). The priests and the cult prophets who had the most to lose were naturally hostile to Jeremiah; the officials of the king's court who were the judges in the proceedings (the "princes") were on Jeremiah's side. The people seem to vacillate—first to the side of the priests, then to the side of the princes—doubtless swayed by the calm assurance of Jeremiah in the face of attack, his willingness to risk his life in speaking the prophetic word, and perhaps also because they understood rightly that Jeremiah's sermon was in reality a promise of God's blessing should Israel turn, repent, and obey God. So the "prophetic" preacher must not be merely fearless in condemnation but also must offer an intense and urgent appeal to new conduct so that the threatened disaster might be averted. Jeremiah was called by Yahweh not only to tear up and break down but also to plant and to build (1:10).

So the preacher might delicately suggest that Simon the Zealot, fierce in his nationalism, was incomplete and in danger of excess until he was tempered by being joined to the number of the twelve. He was zealous now because he was fired with love. The former flames were mastered and controlled for a yet nobler purpose. And Jude by his question (cf. the Gospel, John 14:22) elicited Jesus' saying about the duty of love and obedience so that the Father and Jesus will make their home where love and obedience prevail.

The Episcopal reading is the introduction to the great Song of Moses, inviting the entire world of nature to listen to the word of Yahweh and join in his praise. The theme is so exalted that everyone and everything must pay attention to it. The traditional Gradual for Apostles' Days makes use of Psalm 19 "The heavens declare the glory of God and . . . their sound went forth through all the earth . . ." which joins the Psalm's reference to the testimony of the skies glorifying their Creator with the witness of the Apostles who carried the gospel throughout the known world. Both are reflected in the exalted theology of Rom. 8:19–23 which describes all nature as groaning as it waits for deliverance.

The *Second Lesson:* In the apostolic church it was generally believed that the spirit of prophecy had been revived and that the NT prophets, speaking by the Spirit, revealed hidden truth. As the phenomenon of prophecy spread, the second century church looked for new and ever more startling visions. The question naturally arose, How can one tell a false prophet from a true one? This reading is a warning that there are false prophets in the world and so all prophecy must be tested (cf. 1 Cor. 12:1–11; 1 Thess. 5:19–20). There is here no denial of supernatural spirits. The point is that they can be false or true, evil or holy. One cannot take spiritual phenomena at face value, for deceit is possible and not all religion is good. As the Elder sees it, there is a simple, clearcut distinction: God inspires the orthodox; the devil inspires heretics. The test is whether the prophet acknowledges the incarnation and confesses that Jesus has come "in the flesh," as opposed to a congeries of heresies within the church which denied that Jesus was to be identified completely with Christ. Anyone who denies this, the Elder says, is of the enemy's camp and serves not Christ but Antichrist. In times of crisis such as this in which the second century church found itself, there can be no intermediate position. One must choose sides, and those who refuse to make the choice have sided with the enemy. To be true, therefore, prophecy must be consistent with known revelation (cf. 1 Cor. 12:3).

As there are two kinds of spirits, so there are two kinds of people. The faithful are already victorious, for the Spirit who animates them is greater than the spirit which is in the world, Satan. The division between the world under Satan and the kingdom under God is continued. The world listens to its own spokesmen; the church listens to its own. The world will accept only an easy morality, and the presence of the Antichrist is a sign of the approaching end. The relationship with Jeremiah and the continuity with that prophetic tradition is plain. Jeremiah was despised by the priests who represented the world but was welcomed by those who were of God and who recognized his voice.

The Roman Catholic and Episcopal lesson, an important reading reserved for Sunday in the Lutheran lectionary, is quite different in spirit, speaking not of separation but of the unity which Christ brings. By the cross the distant are made near, the opposed are reconciled. In Christ both Jew and Gentile are at peace with each other in order to create a new sort of person altogether. Walls of separation fall, distinctions disappear. The one living temple of God is the fellowship of the faithful built upon the Apostles and NT prophets—eyewitnesses and interpreters of the gospel—with Christ himself the cornerstone of the building (cf. Isa. 28:16). It is an unusual structure: a growing building, an organic edifice.

This lesson is nonetheless to some degree polemical, for it teaches that the Gentiles are to be incorporated into the "new man" Christ, and the summons, which is not always welcome, is to a new appreciation of the inclusiveness of the church. It is a command to grow. The trinitarian formula inherent in this lesson might also be noted: to the Father, through the Son, in the Spirit.

Taken together, the two Second Lessons from John and Ephesians dialectically present a picture of the church struggling against error and therefore required to make judgments and distinctions, yet called to imitate Christ and therefore required to be accepting. The church is called to see the world both from God's perspective and from our own. As Augustine put it, "Love separates the saints from the world."

The **Gospel** gives the one remark we have from Judas (Jude). As Jesus delivers his last discourse, he is interrupted three times: first by Thomas (14:5), "Lord, how can we know the way?", then by Philip (14:8), "Lord, show us the Father," and this time by Jude, "Lord, how is it that you will manifest yourself to us, and not to the world?" Something more than pure invention by the author seems involved here, for while Thomas and Philip are comparatively vocal in the Fourth Gospel, Jude is entirely unknown except for this question. There may have been some historical basis for attributing the question to him.

The basic question raised by the readings for this feast day is "Why can't it be easier?"—easier to be a faithful spokesman (Jeremiah was threatened with death), easier to tell false from true (the Second Lesson), easier to know Jesus (the Gospel). But, as always, nothing worth having comes easily.

Following Jesus' statement that the world will not see him any more (v. 19), Jude's question is an especially natural one: why doesn't Jesus show himself to the world in one great undeniable epiphany? Then everyone would believe. But belief is not so easily come by. It involves not mere physical seeing (many saw Jesus and did not believe) but a spiritual sight which involves obedience. This loving obedience and obedient love is the vehicle of God's dwelling with people. Then he can make his home with them (cf. 14:1–3; 1:10–18). The Father, and so Jesus and the Paraclete, cannot enter into a relationship with one who refuses to love and obey.

Jesus' strange answer suggests that we are in a realm where human questions have little meaning. Why does God do anything? His ways may seem arbitrary and even unjust, but eventually they do make sense (Rom. 11:32–33). The relationship God intends and requires is one of love and mutual service. Obedience is the proof of love, leading to ever fuller revelation and making possible communion between God and his people. By so loving, people live the life of the Son and so have also the Father and the Spirit come and live in them. God comes to people as the Son, but this is at the same time the coming of the Father and the Paraclete. The fullness of divinity dwells in the Son and also in the believer.

The reading concludes on the note of peace which passes all understanding—the peace which supported Jeremiah during and after the temple sermon, the peace which characterized the second century church under attack by the Antichrist, the peace which always characterizes the church wherever it is found. The manifestation of the Son to each believer is more important here than the parousia for which each must be prepared to wait. In the meantime, peace (cf. the Roman Catholic and Episcopal Second Lesson), harmony, and communion with God are the seal of the covenant.

The Roman Catholic Gospel is Luke's list of the Apostles (which is the Lutheran Gospel for St. Matthias' Day, q.v.). Jesus' choice of the Apostles climaxes the progression of hostility by Jewish leaders and the plot of Jesus' enemies. Luke, who characteristically emphasizes the role of prayer in Jesus' life (cf., e.g., Luke 3:21), has Jesus go to a mountain (cf. Sinai), the scene of great and decisive events in the Gospel, and there pray through the night before making the selection of the twelve from the number of his followers. The choice was a momentous one, taken in the face of mounting hostility, as Jesus formed the nucleus of the new Israel.

Reformation Day

OCTOBER 31

Lutheran	*Pres./UCC/Chr. Ch. (A)*
Jer. 31:31–34*	Hab. 2:1–4†
Rom.Rom. 3:19–28‡	Rom. 3:19–28‡
John 8:31–36	John 8:31–36

The Lutheran Churches have kept various dates in commemoration of the sixteenth century reform of the church. October 31 is the anniversary of Luther's posting the ninety-five theses on the door of the castle church in Wittenberg, questioning excesses in the sale of indulgences. This is the one day on the Lutheran calendar which is peculiar to the Lutheran

* see Lent 5, Series B; Maundy Thursday, Series C   ‡ see Pentecost 2, Series A
† see Pentecost 20, Series C

Church (it is occasionally observed by other Protestant churches), and it has been in the past the occasion of divisive anti-Catholic sermons and demonstrations. Nonetheless, the inclusion of the day in this volume of comments on the Lesser Festivals offers the day to the ecumenical church as a celebration not of division, for that was tragic (though perhaps also a necessity given the times) and nothing to celebrate, but as a celebration of the renewal of the proclamation of the gospel and a recalling of the whole church to its evangelical origins. It is not to be observed as a triumphalist festival as if all error had been purged from the church in 1517, but rather as a day of recalling the revolutionary, cleansing word of God which is constantly renewing and reforming the church. It is a day that reminds the church of the provisional nature of all that is less than God, who in his sovereignty is always free to tear up and destroy in order to build and plant anew. Reform is not a once-for-all event, but rather a permanent state of the church.

The *First Lesson* presents the central and climactic teaching of Jeremiah. The covenant God made with his people at Sinai had been broken by the defection of Israel who had an increasingly limited conception of the law of that covenant. It had become external only, an idol. Jeremiah saw that something more was needed to give people the power to live the life that the covenant required. Cultic reforms under Josiah were short-lived. The prophets made no lasting impression on Israel's conduct.

God, therefore, in the eschatological time promises to cut a new covenant (the expression is the oldest formula for making a covenant) with his people which will give motivation and power to fulfill the law he has already given. He promises to forgive sin and promises that they all will know him, and this forgiveness and knowledge will be the necessary incentive for obeying the law of the Lord. The new covenant, God-centered like the old covenant, thus moved in the realm of personal faith, and the law is no longer a regulation of external activity but is an inspiration of the heart. Its religion was internalized and spiritualized and bore both a personal and a universal character. So the basic requirement of the covenant—"I will be their God and they shall be my people"—will indeed be a reality and people will know Yahweh as the prophets did —directly and intimately in every event and situation. Intermediaries would be useless, for Yahweh will intervene directly.

Yet this renewal of the personal religion is not at the expense of the social aspects of religion, for the new covenant is cut not with individuals but with "the whole house of Israel." Individuals do not exist for themselves alone, but now constitute a people, a house.

The lesson suggests a sermon on the relationship between the old and the new covenants (in Jeremiah's prophecy, in the OT and NT, in Catholicism and Protestantism) in which the old is not abrogated but renewed and deepened as God's people are called to a new perception and apprehension of the heart of what God had done for his people and what he had given them. The lesson is a summons not to divisiveness nor to a near-sighted interiorization but to a renewal of the personal springs of religious devotion from which all righteous works and all social action proceed.

In the Presbyterian, United Church of Christ, and Christian Church lesson, Habakkuk, a contemporary of Jeremiah, voices the impatience of the people who are seeking to understand God's delay in answering their cries. Yahweh's answer is that help is on its way in God's due time. Meanwhile, the unrighteous (that is, the Chaldeans) "shall fail," but the righteous (that is, the Israelites) will live by their faithfulness, by living faithfully, knowing that God's deliverance is on its way. The NT makes wider application of v. 4, "the righteous shall live by his faith": cf. Rom. 1:17; Gal. 3:11; Heb. 10:38–39.

The **Second Lesson** is a classic Pauline passage which sets forth what came to be the heart of the sixteenth century Reformation, contrasting works and faith, the law of God and the righteousness of God. The deeds of the law are actions done in obedience to the law which were regarded by the Jews as a means of attaining righteousness before God. The purpose of the law, however (cf. Gal. 2:16), is to give real and deep knowledge of moral disorder and rebellion against God. For the law demands righteousness but cannot create it. The result, as Paul came to know, is that the law becomes an oppressor.

The revolutionary news is that the way to God comes from God's side and comes as a gift. It is still more shocking than that. God treats the unworthy as if they had been good, and this is contrary to some of the OT (Exod. 23:7; Prov. 17:15). God the angry judge has become the man on the cross, and those estranged from him have become his children. The question is no longer the righteousness of the individual before God, but the righteousness of God which is graciously given to those who have none of their own.

The point to be stressed is not that the redeeming activity of God, described by Paul in terms of the proceedings of a court of law ("justification") is a complete account of all that God does for his people, but that this acquittal that clears the guilt of the accused is the essential element from which all else proceeds. It is not religious systems which save but God himself. Nor is it ultimately institutions, but he whom the institutions embody who is the ground of hope and the source of confidence.

Having thus set his people free from self-serving work in an effort to earn salvation, God, by giving salvation, frees his people for service of one another (cf. Gospel, "free indeed"). This radically democratic principle by which everyone is equal in the sight of God, since all claims to rectitude are excluded, makes each free to offer selfless service. Such an idea is nothing less than a new covenant and such deliverance from slavery to a religious system a new exodus. (The preacher might profitably explore in connection with Reformation Day the recent expressions of "liberation theology" emanating from the minority groups and representatives of the third world.)

Faith itself is no ground for boasting, for it is simply an acknowledgment of the bankruptcy of one's condition before God, of the hopelessness of the situation—unless God chooses to help.

The **Gospel** is a corrective to the mistaken notion that the Second Lesson may seem to foster: that faith is the whole of Christianity, as if believing were sufficient of itself. Having had the question of acceptance by God put into the past as an accomplished fact—since Calvary—the Christian is now free to continue in Jesus' word and to know the truth. Faith, as Paul understands it, is identical with this staying in Jesus' word, making it a settled point of reliance in the life of the believer, a continuing part of his whole personal attitude. Faith too is a living, daring confidence which is a continuing spring of the religious life, which gives shape and texture to one's daily living. It is but the beginning of discipleship, learning, growing, maturing, probing. In the Gospel, the Jews understood the freedom of which Jesus spoke to be spiritual (so they could say they had never been in bondage), but they assumed incorrectly that blood descent gave this freedom to them automatically. Freedom rather is a relationship to God which only God himself can create.

So the Reformation is not a finished fact but a continuing experience of the church, reminding God's people of the continuing strictures of bondage which can seem all too comfortable and yet are less than God: power; forms of church government; formulations of doctrine; worship of ideas rather than God; pride that exalts itself at the expense of others, claiming wisdom but lacking love; divisiveness. The preacher must therefore ask himself and the congregation, What is the besetting sin of this time, this denomination, this congregation?

The Gospel surely must not be the occasion for a diatribe against the

Jews, but rather the opportunity to oppose Christian complacency which presumes upon God's acceptance. Jesus' opponents could not have denied political slavery—Egypt, Babylonia, Rome. The Jews were in fact descendants of Abraham through Isaac the free-born (and not through the slave-born Ishmael, Gen. 17:21). But this noble tradition had been compromised by sin and they had, despite their heritage, become slaves. Those who had been chosen now found themselves outside. As in the political sphere, spiritual freedom is easily lost, and its price is eternal vigilance. The sense of responsibility that is concomitant with sonship easily gives way to assuming a rather automatic divine protection. Freedom is self-forgetful service, the inseparable companion of truth. Self-love imprisons the soul; it is set free by the love of God, "whose service is perfect freedom."

All Saints' Day

NOVEMBER 1

Lutheran	*Roman Catholic*	*Episcopal*
Isa. 26:1–4, 8–9, 12–13, 19–21	Rev. 7:2–4, 9–14*	Ecclus. 44:1–10, 13–14
Rev. 21:9–11, 22–27, (22:1–5)†	1 John 3:1–3‡	Rev. 7:9–17*
Matt. 5:1–12§	Matt. 5:1–12a§	Matt. 5:1–12§

This feast, commemorating all the saints of God, known and unknown, began in the West with the consecration of the rebuilt pantheon in Rome as a Christian Church, dedicated to St. Mary and All Martyrs, May 13, 609/610. Gregory III (d. 741) on November 1 dedicated a chapel in St. Peter's basilica to all the saints, and in 835 Gregory IV made the observance of that date as All Saints' Day universal in the Western Church. In the East, the saints are remembered on the first Sunday after Pentecost, and the commemoration dates from the fourth century.

As the feast has expanded from a commemoration of all martyrs to a commemoration of all saints, it has taken on new dimensions. It is in effect a feast of the church, militant and triumphant, and it calls to mind the size and the solidarity of the people of God—a vast community that spreads beyond all bounds of race and language and condition, beyond

* see Easter 4, Series C   ‡ see Easter 4, Series B
† see Easter 6, Series C   § see Epiphany 4, Series A

even time and space, across the divide of death. In each faithful person the Christian proclamation has concrete realization (cf. the Gospel for SS. Simon and Jude). When we praise the saints we praise God himself who has triumphed through them and whose abounding grace we see in their lives.

The day comes at the end of the church year as an anticipation of the coming kingdom and toward the close of the secular year at a time when in the mists and frosts of late autumn spirits were often thought to be about.

The *First Lesson* in the Lutheran lectionary is a series of verses (the condemnatory passages are excised) from a psalm of victory and rejoicing, which invites trust in God, followed by an apocalyptic section with an eschatological expectation.

The first section (vv. 1–4) is a song of praise appropriate for use upon entering Jerusalem to celebrate a victory (cf. Ps. 24:7–10). Zion is a strong city (cf. Ps. 48:13–14)—as opposed to the city of chaos (24:10)—and the victorious nation asks admission with a statement of God's faithfulness (v. 3) and a call to trust forever (v. 4) in God who brings down the citadel of the enemy (v. 4; cf. Obadiah 3).

The second section (vv. 8–9, 12–13, 19) changes to a mood of supplication (similar to a psalm of entreaty; cf. Psalms 44, 60, 74) in which the congregation proclaims its loyalty to God, whose name they remember with gratitude and confidence for what he has done ("memorial name"). Israel has been ruled by aliens, yet the people acknowledge only the rule of God. Even though they are like dead people, God will raise them to life and bring light to the land of the shadow of gloom, despair, and death (cf. Ps. 23:4). As the dew revives the parched vegetation, the nation will be restored to life in a national revival (cf. Ezekiel 37). Perhaps there is the additional implication here of the resurrection of the individual faithful dead (cf. Dan. 12:2–3)—the enemies are to remain dead (v. 14)—a doctrine of late Judaism (second century B.C.). Such may have been the comfort of a broken and depopulated nation: there will be a vast number of people to celebrate and share in the victory of Yahweh.

These verses at times recall the beatitudes (vv. 8–9 are similar to Matt. 5:6; v. 12 is similar to Matt. 5:9) as well as the whole sense of fulfillment of earthly status in the kingdom.

Vv. 20–21 are Yahweh's oracular answer to the preceding psalms. The victory sung in the psalms is not yet. The people can only wait until Yahweh comes from his place. He is even now on his way; the time of waiting will not be long. Then justice will be meted out and violence and its effects will be no longer hidden from God the righteous judge. Even the ancient sin of Cain (Gen. 4:8–12) will be exposed and the voice of Abel's blood (cf. Luke 11:51) heard and requited.

The Episcopal lesson is the magnificent praise of famous and devout ancestors from Ecclesiasticus 44, which substantiates the author's thesis that true wisdom resides in Israel. A devout Jew of the second century B.C. reviews the history of his people. Rulers and counsellors and teachers and composers and landowners: the names of some are still remembered, the names of others long since lost. Those whose names live on are praised in the succeeding chapters of Ecclesiasticus. The introductory passage is a reminder of the number and diversity of our devout ancestors—Christian and Jewish—and tells something of the size and nature of that part of the church which has gone before us. Many are now forgotten by us, unknown to us, but all are remembered by God and so live in him.

The Roman Catholic reading, which is paralleled by the Episcopal Second Lesson, is another traditional expression of the immensity of the company of heaven. An angel comes from the east, the direction of the rising sun from which the Messiah was expected, and calls for a stay of judgment until the chosen are identified. The sacred number of completeness, twelve (twelve tribes, twelve apostles) is multiplied by itself and then by a thousand. There are twelve thousand from each tribe, the spiritual Israel (beginning with Judah, Jesus' tribe) and after them a "great multitude which no man could number" stands and sings. Not one of the redeemed is missing. The martyrs (v. 14) stand clothed in righteousness holding palms of victory, and they sing to the enthroned God and the Lamb. The angels reply with a seven-fold ascription of praise, ending as it began, "Amen.'" The 144,000 martyrs are sealed by the living God: they belong to him and are under his protection. Those who have died are marked by God as his own, as those who have been baptized have been sealed with the Spirit as children in the family of God.

The **Second Lesson**: Carried by an angel (cf. 17:1) to the top of a mountain (cf. Ezek. 40:2), the revelator has an intense ecstatic experience: a vision of the purified and renewed city of God, the new Jerusalem, bright with God's presence and glory. In this gem-like luminary city there is no need for the temple (cf. John 4:21). The place of sacrifice is replaced by the presence and the glory of God and the Lamb (cf. Heb. 9: 23-28). The glorified city is a place of light and purity (cf. Isa. 60:1, 19); perhaps John is suggesting that the astrological deities have been replaced by God and Christ. There is no night, no fear, no reason to shut the gates (cf. Isa. 60:11).

Moreover, unlike old Jerusalem, there is an adequate water supply, for the river of life (cf. Ps. 46:4) flows through the midst of the city, fresh and never-failing (cf. Gen. 2: 8-13; 3:22; Ezek. 47:1-12). In this paradise (the garden of Genesis has given way to an ideal city) the tree of life becomes many trees with an abundance of life (cf. Ezek. 47:7), and they grow by the river. Their fruit is good for food, and the leaves are good for healing. The saints and the Lamb and God are joined in the perfect service of praise. The culmination is the sight of the face of God, the beatific vision (cf. 1 Cor. 13:12; Matt. 5:8, "They shall see God"). The progression is from the OT hope to the sight of Jesus by the eyewitness to the faith of those who follow in later ages to the beatific vision.

The Roman Catholic lesson, 1 John 3:1–3, weaves together teaching and behavior and draws out the ethical implications of the visions of the consummation. God's love, which made us his children, produces an increasing resemblance to him (cf. 2 Cor. 3:18) until the resemblance is complete (cf. Phil. 3:21; Rom. 8:19, 23) and we are as he wants us to be. Then we shall see him as he is: the beatific vision of Revelation 22 (cf. Matt. 5:8). The reference in the first verse to "children of God" connects with the Gospel (Matt. 5:9); a present reality points to eschatological fulfillment.

The **Gospel** in all three lectionaries is the Beatitudes which summarize the new spirit of the kingdom of God and proclaim God's favor to those who seek to live under his rule. In the basic NT sense a "saint" is a believer, one made holy by the Spirit of God, part of God's "holy nation."

The setting is important. Jesus on the hill teaches his disciples in the presence of the crowds (cf. Matt. 28:19–20; the disciples are to go and teach all nations, and through their teaching the voice of Jesus is heard; he teaches the nations through them). So too the movement of this section of the Great Sermon (which is doubtless the evangelist's compilation and arrangement of brief, originally separate sayings) is from the general addresses of vv. 3–10 ("Blessed are . . .") to the direct personal application of vv. 11–12 ("Blessed are you. . . .") The early church no doubt heard the voice of Jesus in these latter verses speaking to it in times of persecution. Not only present disciples but also those who become Jesus' disciples in the future receive the same promises and blessings. The continuity is stressed which joins the biblical period with the apostolic age and with all succeeding time. The voice of Jesus is still heard, teaching and commanding and blessing.

So on All Saints' Day, the ordinary Christian sits on the Mount at Jesus' feet with the crowds, listening to him talking to and through his smaller band of selected ones. Many are called to be Christians, but only a few are of a conspicuous sanctity, in whom love has clearly made his home. And it is through them that we learn what we might become.

But the company of saints is a diverse and multi-textured fellowship. As the church recalls with thanksgiving the lives of saintly women and men, both known and unknown, she reads the beatitudes which tell of the kinds of people who are blessed in the kingdom of God. It is a repudiation of the values of the world, and those who do not share those values and who suffer from their practice are blessed in the kingdom.

The first four beatitudes deal with those who are aware of their emptiness and that of the world. They tell of the absolute dependence of the last who will eventually be first: the lowly, the little ones, the destitute, and the outcast (cf. 1 Cor. 1:26–29). Blessed are the oppressed who know their need of God (the "poor" including those who are literally poverty-stricken); the mourners who lament the disobedience to God by a passing world (cf. Isa. 61:2); the humble who come to God with empty hands (cf. Ps. 37:11); the hungry for right who pray earnestly for the coming kingdom and the vindication of God's purpose (cf. 8:11).

The next three beatitudes deal with the disciples who show positive, active qualities appropriate to the kingdom of God: the forgiving who display the character of God (cf. 18:21); the pure and single-minded who are free from mixed motives (cf. Ps. 24:3–4; 51:10; 73:1); the makers of peace who help to create the condition in which the kingdom can grow (cf. 5:44 ff.); and those who thus participate in the peace which passes understanding (Phil. 4:7).

The final beatitudes turn to the listener and make a personal application of the general statements of beatitude. The blessed in the kingdom, such as have been described, are always ready to suffer gladly for their revolutionary attitude (cf. 1 Pet. 3:14; 4:14), for persecution is part of their calling. In so doing the disciples will follow in the succession of the prophets who in times past were God's messengers (cf. 2 Chron. 36:15–16; Matt. 10:41; 13:17; 23:34–37; Acts 7:52). The eighth beatitude returns to the promise of the first, rounding off the general statements which describe those who are in the kingdom. The suffering of the disciples is the proof that they will share the kingdom.

Thanksgiving Day

Lutheran	Roman Catholic (after harvest)	Episcopal	Pres./UCC/Chr. Ch.
Deut. 8:1–10	Deut. 8:7–18	Deut. 8:6–11	Deut. 8:6–17 (C)
Phil. 4:6–20* or	1 Tim. 6:6–11, 17–19	James 1:16–21	1 Tim. 2:1–8 (A)†
1 Tim. 2:1–4†			Luke 17:11–19 (B)‡
Luke 17:11–19‡	Luke 17:11–19‡	Matt. 6:25–33§	

The OT has elaborate regulations governing the offering of sacrifices of thanksgiving, and the impulse to display gratitude in ritual is very ancient in world religion. The harvest was generally celebrated throughout Europe on November 11 (St. Martin's Day), and the goose, especially in Holland, was the traditional meal.

In America the Pilgrims celebrated a three-day thanksgiving in 1621 with goose and turkey and beer. The second thanksgiving day was celebrated July 30, 1623. The observance became general in New England, and in 1665 Connecticut appointed an annual day of thanksgiving on the last Wedneseday in October. George Washington proclaimed November 26, 1789 as a day of national thanksgiving for the adoption of the Constitution. Local dates were observed, especially in New England, until 1863 when Abraham Lincoln set the last Thursday in November as an annual day of thanksgiving to God for the blessings of the year. From 1939–1941, Thanksgiving was observed on the third Thursday in November (to extend the Christmas shopping time), but because of opposition Congress by a joint resolution set the fourth Thursday in November as the day. It has lost most of its overtones of a harvest festival and is instead a day of general thanksgiving for God's blessings to the nation.

Canada first observed a day of thanksgiving November 6, 1879. Following World War I, the day was combined with Armistice Day and celebrated on the Monday of the week in which November 11 occurred. It is now fixed by annual proclamation as the second Monday in October.

The primary activity on Thanksgiving Day should naturally be praise and thanksgiving, hymns and prayers. But some sort of homily or com-

---

* see Pentecost 20 and 21, Series A
† see Pentecost 18, Series C
‡ see Pentecost 21, Series C
§ see Epiphany 4, Series A

ment on the readings is also appropriate. The *First Lesson* is an appeal to Israel's memory of God's care during the time in the wilderness, and its extended form (Roman Catholic and Presbyterian/United Church of Christ/Christian Church) includes a warning against a proud sense of self-sufficiency which ignores Israel's dependency upon Yahweh. As Israel prepares to enter the promised land, "the commandment" (i.e., 6:4–19; see also 10:12–22; 11:22—loving and obeying Yahweh) is solemnly laid upon them in grand oratorical style.

The central phrase is "you shall remember"; the memory is to be kept alive and nourished. Here, as throughout the Bible, "remember" implies more than recalling. By memory the past is kept alive, continuity is maintained with the formative experiences of the nation, and the past is made a contemporary experience of the community. The people thus are to remember the time of testing in the wilderness and the lesson of the manna that Israel was to live not only by that gift of grace but by everything that comes from God. They are entirely dependent upon him. The hardship of the wandering had a providential disciplinary purpose to purify and strengthen and teach the people (cf. Hos. 11; Heb. 12:3–11), to humble Israel's pride and test the quality of their faith. But the grace which imposed the discipline also supplied the means to endure the discipline—the manna. And the grace became yet more abundant when the people entered upon the riches of the land of promise.

The purpose of the testing ultimately was to prepare for entrance into the good land of promise which would supply their every need. The nomadic tribes are about to enter a developed agricultural country of great promise. (The similarity to the people who came to North America and found here a great and rich land is plain.)

But there is more to be said than "Bless the Lord," for with great possessions comes the temptation to ignore him who is the source of all that is good. The providential direction of the wanderings obliges Israel to obey the whole of God's commands. When they are settled in the land and when they enjoy its richness, they are not to think that they do not need God any longer, nor are they to miss the abounding testimony to his goodness. They must not forget the path that got them to this place; they must remember the whole story of the cost: the possession, the discipline, and the gift. Their history is to be rehearsed and renewed constantly so that they do not forget.

The lesson suggests a fruitful approach to the theme of thanksgiving. It obviously does no good to command people to "Be thankful," although it is often done nonetheless. Instead, a review of the great acts of history by which the nation came into being but for which the nation is not inclined to be especially grateful is indicated. The preacher must be careful to be specific and to avoid cliches, for it is this review of the past mercy of God that gives confidence for the future. It is this God who keeps his promises.

The Second Lesson and the Gospel are essentially lessons in prayer. The *Second Lesson*, from the cordial, affectionate, and radiantly joyful letter to the Philippians, invites a consideration of the relationship between thanksgiving and prayer, suggesting that an attitude of thanksgiving is basic and essential for prayer. The ungrateful person cannot pray.

Paul was in prison when he wrote this letter, but even there as his understanding of himself and of God grew, so did his sense of obligation. Gratitude and commitment go hand in hand. Gratitude leads to thanksgiving and thanksgiving leads to submission to the will of God. So the result of prayer is "that peace which the world cannot give"—not a deliverance from trouble (Paul remains in prison) but a deliverance from self-serving.

Paul's list of the fine things one ought to think about can be understood here as an invitation to give thanks for particular examples one sees (let the preacher be specific) of the true, which does not deceive; the worthy that has the dignity of holiness upon it; the righteous; the undefiled and winsome that calls forth love; the things which are fit for God to hear. None of these virtues is surprising in the light of the OT or of Greek philosophy. The suggestion is that what is distinctive about the Christian life, finally, is not the particular manifestation but the motive—gratitude for God's grace.

Before the letter ends, Paul thanks the Philippians for a tangible gift of money that they had sent to him by Epaphroditus. Their circumstances had changed and such a gift was now possible. Paul understands, and he could, if it had been necessary, have managed without their gift, for he had learned the secret of contentment in whatever circumstance he found himself (cf. Roman Catholic lesson). The gift that the Philippians sent was an offering not to Paul but to God who will supply everything they need. Their generosity made Paul happy, not for himself but for their sake. They had grown in Christian love. So thanksgiving is not simply offering thanks, but it is also the giving of gifts as one opens oneself more and more to the gifts and riches of God.

The Lutheran alternate lesson, 1 Tim. 2:1–4, tells of the universal relevance of Christianity, answering the basic question, Should Christians pray for heathen rulers, particularly the Roman emperor? with a firm Yes. God wants everyone to come to a knowledge of the truth.

The Roman Catholic lesson, 1 Tim. 6:6–11, 17–19, praises moderation, Christian contentment, for possessions distract from the center of life (cf. 2 Cor. 9:8) which is God, who gives us richly everything to enjoy. Paul does not condemn wealth but emphasizes its dangers and stresses the true riches in the world to come which follow from wealth in good deeds in this world.

The Episcopal lesson is a statement that God is the source of all good gifts. God is the Father of the lights of heaven (sun, moon, and stars) which are the prime examples of the good gifts he has given, together with life (the original creation) and the word of truth (the gospel).

The *Gospel* of the grateful Samaritan presents Jesus as the beneficent healer who lavishes his goodness upon all who are in need and who receives thanks from the one foreigner. The poignant question, "Where are the nine?" echoes through this story. But the preacher needs to do more than condemn those nine who were not apparently grateful and to pity Jesus standing pathetic and forlorn, for the real victims of ingratitude are these nine.

It was no mistake to cure ten; that is God's lavish mercy at work. He blesses, heals, restores health even when that amazing grace will be taken for granted. Those who did not respond to this richly overflowing love closed the door to further gifts. The one Samaritan did resepond and received a further blessing: "Your faith has made you whole." More than a mere cure, this one who was ready and open received the gift of wholeness. His entire life had been put back together again.

It is more than a matter of etiquette and saying "Thank you." The Gospel goes deeper and tells of gratitude which is the basis for receiving a whole new way of life. The Gospel teaches response to what God has done so he can do still more. The nine went back to their original life presumably healed; the Samaritan began a yet fuller life in a new relationship with God in his kingdom, proclaiming the redemptive acts in the midst of his people.

The Episcopal Gospel, Matt. 6:25–33, describes the life that is free from care. God who gives life can be trusted to give lesser things as well. Worry is essentially distrust of God, for a Christian who knows God as a loving Father finds worry impossible. Moreover, worry comes from putting oneself in the center rather than God's kingdom (cf. Isa. 26:3). Confidence comes from a knowledge of the nature of God who knows intimately the needs of his children. So the "Franciscan element" of biblical religion impels one to a joyous abandon to God, for one must come to terms with one's material life in order to learn to pray.

This Gospel urges a sense of proportion that sees things in their proper perspective. Food and clothing are of less importance than life, and the kingdom of God is more important than life. Until the kingdom of God is given its rightful place, nothing else can be understood or valued properly. We pray "Your kingdom come" before we pray "Give us today. . . ." And Jesus not only taught but lived that prayer.

National Holiday

Lutheran	*Episcopal*	*Pres./UCC/Chr. Ch.*
Jer. 29:4–14	Isa. 26:1–8	Isa. 26:1–8 (B)
Rom. 13:1–10*	Rom. 13:1–10*	Rom. 13:1–8 (A)*
Mark 12:13–17	Mark 12:13–17	Mark 12:13–17 (B)

The provision of propers for a National Holiday is new to the Lutheran tradition in America, which had stressed the church's year without regard to the days of the nation in which the church found itself. In practice, however, many congregations observe the holidays of the nation in one way or another, particularly (in the United States) Memorial Day, Independence Day, and Labor Day. The new Lutheran lectionary, therefore, together with the Episcopal and Presbyterian/United Church of Christ/ Christian Church calendars, provides propers for a day of civic or national significance following the advice given in 1 Tim. 2:1–4.

The *First Lesson* in the Lutheran lectionary is from a letter sent by Jeremiah to the exiles in in Babylonia apparently just after the exile began (598 B.C.). It was carried by Elash and Gemariah, envoys of King Zedekiah, who were taking tribute of vassalage to the Babylonian king. The exiles had been led to believe that they would soon return to their homeland. Jeremiah wrote to correct this false hope, and his advice was startling: they were to build homes in Babylonia, settle in, plant gardens, marry; and, what was yet more revolutionary, they were to work for the good of Babylonia and make their contribution to its welfare. The verses of the letter from which this lesson is taken are, it seems, quite genuine. It is one of the most significant documents in the OT, for it sug-

* see Pentecost 16, Series A

gests that God is not limited to the temple nor even to the promised land. The people were not to be deceived with illusions of an early return to their own land, for there would be no return until Yahweh's purpose had been accomplished. Even though the exile must last seventy years, nonetheless the plans of God are for his people's good. He will not forget them in a strange land.

The reading sets the theme for the relationship between the church and the nation. It is not to be an easy symbiosis. Always the tension of a church in the world but not of the world must be maintained. This does not mean an otherworldly isolation, for the church, like the exiles in Babylonia, is here for an extended stay; and all the responsibilities of citizens are to be fulfilled, as the exiles work for the welfare of the nation. Yet this does not mean an entirely comfortable relationship, for the church must always bear in mind its exile status; while it bears responsibility to the world, its real home is elsewhere.

The church, therefore, celebrates national holidays with some reluctance; Christians participate in them gladly as citizens, yet the church is unwilling to suggest that the purposes of the state and the purposes of the church are exactly the same. The two kingdoms interpenetrate dialectically, each teaching and correcting the other; but they are not to be confused.

The Episcopal and Presbyterian/United Church of Christ/Christian Church lesson, Isa. 26:1–9, must therefore be read with care, lest the opening verses seem to commend the present nation as "the righteous nation which keeps faith." The song of victory of which these verses are a part is an eschatological vision of the working out of God's justice. Before the entrance of the righteous nation can take place, pride must be crushed (cf. Obadiah 3) and the poor exalted (vv. 5–6). The preacher must also guard against excessively privatizing "peace" as if personal spiritual harmony were all that mattered. But the "peace" of v. 3 is also to be distinguished from world concord which is brought about by the concerted will of the nations—whatever their religious majority—to walk the path of peace (cf. Luke 1:79).

The **Second Lesson** is the classic NT description of the responsibility of the church to the state (assuming that "the governing authorities" is the state and not the angelic powers as in Col. 1:16). God, who brought order out of chaos, continues to rule his creation. Government is instituted by him as an aspect and image of his providential care of what he has made and over which he rules. Rulers, therefore, must reflect and participate in the lordship of God (cf. Wisd. 6:3). Without rule and order, there would be chaos. Not only has government in general been instituted by God, but all existing authority has been instituted by him. Resistance to this lordship then is disobedience of God.

Paul's experience with the Roman Empire was largely positive; he was proud to be a citizen (Acts 22:27–28). Even when the persecution began, Christians continued to counsel obedience and respect for civil authority (cf. Titus 3:1; 1 Pet. 2:13–17) and prayers for the government continued. Nor was Paul entirely unaware of the potential persecution already present in the world (cf. Rom. 8:35–38). Moreover, he gave this counsel in chap. 13, presumably because it needed to be said, for the desire to throw off all earthly and pagan restraint must have been intense.

It needs to be remembered that the ruler who is to be obeyed is at the same time himself under God and under a command to obey him. God is "the Power" (cf. Mark 14:62), and all other power is derivative from him. So the view expressed in Acts 5:29, "We must obey God rather than men," must be set beside this counsel of obedience. When the Christians obeyed the ruler, they were not obeying a man but God. When the state commanded idolatry, as in the worship of the emperors, Christians refused to obey chiefly because of their larger view of God as the real ruler of heaven and earth, who would not work through earthly rulers to contradict himself. God was not ruling through these men who were blind to their obligations before God. Thus Tertullian could declare, "Caesar is more ours than yours because our God appointed him."

As in the First Lesson, so here the thought is that one cannot dissociate oneself from the society in which he lives. As citizenship in the nation gives certain benefits which the individual alone cannot enjoy, so with the benefits one must also accept the duties. Taxes are to be paid (cf. the Gospel).

The lesson continues beyond the particular verses associated with civil authority to vv. 8–10 which tell of love being the fulfillment of the law (or "Love is the law in all its fullness"). It is a useful reminder that Christian duty does not end with the discharge of civil obligation. One expects no more (nor less) than justice from the state, but for Christians love is also required, and that love is to be all inclusive and not directed only to Christians. Again, the church is reminded of its status in the world, yet there is more, for it is not of the world.

The *Gospel* deals with a difficult and important question of Jesus' day. The Herodian party, the chief priests, and the Sadducean nobility contended that taxes ought to be paid. The Pharisees, while longing for a time when they would no longer be under the Roman rule, kept the peace by paying the taxes. Rebellion had been tried and failed (cf. Acts 5:37), but the Zealots, who were growing in popularity, were calling for new rebellion against the subjugation to Rome.

The tax in question was a poll tax equal to a day's wage and was extremely unpopular because it was a reminder of the Jews' subjugation and because the coin by which it was paid was a graven image of the emperor with his claim to divinity inscribed on it. The question then that was put to Jesus was carefully cast so as to trap Jesus no matter which way he answered it.

His answer begins with the acknowledgment that since the money is Caesar's, it belongs to him. Taxes should be paid. But Jesus' real point is the contrast between Caesar and God. Political power is insignificant when compared with the kingdom of heaven. Caesar can be paid easily with his own money. But what God requires (cf. Mic. 6:8) involves all of one's being and a lifetime of service. A small coin symbolized the empire of Caesar; the universe was the kingdom of God. Caesar's image is seen in a coin; God's image is seen in his people. "To Caesar what is Caesar's; to God what is God's." The saying came to have particular significance to Christians during the persecution under Nero in A.D. 64. Even the endurance of suffering and death was a small price to pay for a lasting crown of glory in a kingdom that has no end.